We're On Your Side!

We're On Your Side!

A Message From Managers

Kim D. Ward
Thomas Cooke

iUniverse, Inc.

New York Lincoln Shanghai

We're On Your Side!
A Message From Managers

iUniverse books may be ordered through booksellers or by contacting:

iUniverse
2021 Pine Lake Road, Suite 100
Lincoln, NE 68512
www.iuniverse.com
1-800-Authors (1-800-288-4677)

ISBN-13: 978-0-595-39432-6 (pbk)
ISBN-13: 978-0-595-67705-4 (cloth)
ISBN-13: 978-0-595-83828-8 (ebk)
ISBN-10: 0-595-39432-9 (pbk)
ISBN-10: 0-595-67705-3 (cloth)
ISBN-10: 0-595-83828-6 (ebk)

Printed in the United States of America

Contents

About the Authors vii

Introduction ix

Foreword—A Message From Your Managers xi

Getting Started: Instructions and Applications xiii

Chapter 1   Dare to Dream 1

Chapter 2   Creating Your Future 6

Chapter 3   Planning For Success 14

Chapter 4   The Value of Position Descriptions 22

Chapter 5   Winning Behavior 28

Chapter 6   The Greatest Gift 35

Chapter 7   Successful Leveraging 41

Chapter 8   Mutual Commitments 47

Chapter 9   Developing Resources 53

Chapter 10 Choosing Priorities 59

Chapter 11 Decisions That Pay 68

Chapter 12 Focusing Your Energy 74

Chapter 13 Understanding Change 82

Chapter 14 Working With Change 90

Chapter 15 Creating Change 97

The Final Plan—Action Mapping 103

Quick Quote Reference Guide 113

Research References: 119

About the Authors

Kim D. Ward

Kim D. Ward is the Director of Education and Training with LEARNING OUTSOURCE GROUP, an international provider of learning solutions dedicated to helping their clients build and sustain competitive advantage. He has been involved in the training and consulting industry in a variety of capacities since 1990. His expertise encompasses training needs analysis and assessment, business/process re-organization, consulting, curriculum development and training facilitation. Kim has been instrumental in helping numerous organizations achieve and exceed sales growth and profitability objectives. Kim has authored and co-authored numerous training programs including *Leading High Velocity Change* and *C³ Partnering for Success*. His last book, *Decisions Without Mistakes (Common Sense Decision Making Strategies for Today's Managers and Leaders)* was released in December 2002.

Kim has personally delivered seminars to over 100,000 participants. His professional presence, personal success and ability to engage his audience has earned him an excellent reputation in several industries including communications, finance, technology and e-commerce, automotive, office automation and distribution. He serves on Ohio University's Sales Centre Professional Sales Advisory Board and has over 25 years of sales, management and executive leadership experience. He resides with his family in Longwood, Florida.

Thomas Cooke

Thomas Cooke is the founder and president of LEARNING OUTSOURCE GROUP. As an internationally recognized speaker and facilitator since 1992, he has been a featured speaker at numerous executive leadership conferences for a variety of organizations. He has authored or co-authored various training programs including *Sales Management Leadership in the 21st Century*. Thousands of managers and executives from over 20 countries have participated in programs he has created or facilitated during the past decade. He is considered an authority in Sales Education and Sales Management Leadership Development.

Tom has a Bachelors Degree from Ohio University in Economics and completed post-graduate studies at Georgia State University. He serves on Ohio University's Sales Centre Professional Sales Advisory Board and is currently involved with several major universities conducting research and publications on Sales Management Effectiveness. He is also a member of ASTD and numerous other civic and professional organizations. He resides in Daytona Beach, Florida.

Introduction

To hard working employees everywhere:

You are about to embark on a powerful journey. This voyage will take you from where you are today to where you'd like to be in your future. We all possess the potential to achieve tremendous levels of success and happiness in any area of our life. All we need to do is capitalize on our true potential.

Our potential is the foundation on which success can be built

Unfortunately, many people never employ the necessary tools that must be utilized in order to reach these possible heights of personal satisfaction, accomplishment and financial reward. It could be they were never given the appropriate tools. Maybe they simply didn't understand the value of the tools when they saw them.

Most people realize their job is the primary source of income and their hope is this income will propel them into a desirable and fulfilling future. And yet a large number of workers struggle to summon up the daily motivation to go to work. According to an independent survey of working Americans, more than 70% of them would like to achieve greater levels of satisfaction at work.

So, why aren't more people completely happy on their jobs?

You don't know what you don't know…you know?

We believe the primary causes of these issues are a lack of information, education, mentorship, planning, execution and reinforcement. Even with the best intentions, if you lack the necessary attitudes, strategies and tools, less complicated working conditions as well as higher levels of satisfaction and achievement may remain out of reach. We would like to help everyone improve his or her posture in life. Our commitment is to continue to find ways for you to take more control of your future and your happiness so you can provide greater opportunities for your family and yourself.

In order to accelerate and accomplish this important improvement transition we must consider the attitudes and strategies that work best in today's world. We must educate ourselves to create reasonable opportunities and take advantage of the information and growth possibilities we now have available. We should look to employees who continue to strive for and reach their potential and follow their successful examples. We must create plans for ourselves that will continue to guide and direct us on our chosen path to enrichment. And, we need to reinforce our good work with an appreciation and celebration of our achievements along the way to our desired future. We all have the ability to accomplish our goals with a lot less pain and a lot more gain.

Success is nothing more than the inevitable outcome of a life lived to it's fullest potential

This book contains the collective experiences, efforts and expertise of many successful people we have had the honor to know. As managers ourselves, we are continually concerned for the employees we are fortunate enough to manage and lead. We believe many of the managers you know care about you as well.

We're On Your Side, is written from the manager's point of view in an effort to help you understand how, with your good intentions and work, and their assistance, your time at work can become less complicated and more fulfilling. Please consider allowing these pages to serve as a working toolkit, which can't be found in any school or many homes. These tools have been proven to help any person who possesses the desire to get more out of themselves and their work to achieve the levels of happiness and success that eludes so many people.

It's really up to you!

Sincerely,

Kim D. Ward and Thomas Cooke

We're On Your Side!

A Message From Your Managers:

We think the time has come for us to speak out and make our collective minds known to our employees.

We know how difficult it is to be an employee today. Keep in mind that we are also employees. We may have different job titles, roles and responsibilities but like you, we are employees.

We labor with some decisions the way that you do. We care about our clients and customers just like you. We love and support our families the same as you. We serve in our communities and places of worship. We play games, take vacations with our loved ones, have fun, face hardships, win and lose just like you.

The only real difference between us is that in addition to our role as an employee we have also accepted the position and responsibility of manager. We are your managers.

We understand that you must sometimes think of us as different. You may view us as outsiders because we sometimes use language that may be foreign to you. Perhaps we seem preoccupied or distant at times. We are often overheard using phrases like, bottom line, market share, turnover, margins, budgets, return on investment and profit potential. We utilize unfamiliar tools like position descriptions, tactical maps, effectiveness assessments and development plans.

Even though all of these things may cause us to appear to be different, there are many more things that make us alike. The most important similarity is that we also care about you!

We believe that with the role of manager comes great responsibility. We believe that all employees deserve great leadership. We honestly hope that all of our employees will have their personal and professional needs met on the job. We would like to see everyone fulfilled and become successful based on his or her own definitions of success and fulfillment. We care about every, single one of you and we wish you nothing but the best.

We would like to cross the chasm that sometimes exists between you as employees and us as managers. We'd prefer to further develop integrity and trust in our relationships with you. We hope to help you discover and define your own future, whether you decide that future is here with us or somewhere down a different path. We'll attempt to prepare you for any goal or task that you may set for yourself. We'd like to simplify your life, not complicate it. It's important to us that you travel home at the end of every day knowing that you've been successful at work and that you have made headway toward the direction you've chosen for yourself. We hope to instill in you an understanding of the value and power of teamwork. We'd like to reduce stress and anxiety for you at work. We envision a workplace environment where you actually look forward to spending your time. We desire for you to be happy here. We believe that our company's only sustainable advantage is you and your co-workers. We believe in you!

This book is from us to you! We hope that you will open your mind and heart to the sincerity of our good intentions toward you. We believe that if you will allow us to help you and, if you'll work with us, that we can guide you in getting more of what you want out of your professional life, your personal goals and your relationships at work. We would like to ensure for you more true satisfaction in what has been possibly, up to now…just another job.

We believe that, if you'll take the time to read this book and work through the exercises, it will aid you in becoming more successful in the work and life that you choose for yourself. We are prepared to enthusiastically assist you in this effort.

Please believe that in our heart of hearts we wish only the best for you and that…

We're on your side!

Respectfully,

Your Managers

Getting Started:
Instructions and Applications

So you may receive the greatest possible benefits this book has to offer please consider the following instruction and application suggestions.

This book was created with the reader in mind. It has been specifically designed and written as an ongoing, weekly personal study and improvement process. People don't usually get the way they are over night. We get the way we are over time. If we are going to change ourselves and/or our condition for the better then we need an improvement plan, which allows us to slowly and deliberately, make sustainable changes in ourselves and for ourselves over time.

Suggestions:

1. Each chapter is designed to take between 20 and 40 minutes to read.
2. Read each chapter and complete the chapter exercises and worksheets as indicated and explained.
3. After completing each individual chapter, consider reviewing your thoughts and work with your manager and anyone else who might care about you, your success and your future. *(Creating and building liaisons of support will help you to make stronger commitments to yourself as you make improvements going forward.)*
4. Once you have completed the primary 15 chapters, read and complete the Final Plan—Action Mapping section by following the exercise instructions contained there.
5. Consider reviewing your final plans with your support liaisons one last time to solidify your intentions and plans for self-improvement.

As you read and work through this book keep this thought in mind:

If it's going to be...it's up to me!

Thank you for your commitment to personal excellence and good fortune!

Chapter 1

Dare to Dream

As you travel the road of life you may find this statement to be true.

A successful person will take responsibility for what needs to be done...and do it

The challenge is, many people are working very hard, attempting to do the right things, all the while losing sight of why they were willing to accept the responsibility in the first place.

More people today are having greater difficulty imagining any long-term future inside their current company. According to *The Herman Group*, creator of *The Herman Trend Alert*, several recent studies suggest as many as 40 percent of American workers have mentally "checked out" of their job. These studies also suggest more than half of American workers are at some level dissatisfied with their current job. Wow! How can such a large percentage of American workers be somewhat dissatisfied with a job most of them applied for and were subsequently hired for?

Finding answers involves understanding the questions

There are many reasons for the dissatisfaction so many Americans feel. Some of these reasons are:

1. Changing business environments
2. Competitive job markets
3. Corporate reorganizations
4. Mergers/acquisitions
5. Changing technology

6. Increased personal economic pressures

7. Poor or slow communications

8. Unfocused work energy

In order to begin the process of creating and achieving reasonable satisfaction in our work life, we must work for what we believe are important reasons. If we are to actuate our journey and achieve reasonable satisfaction from working we should first attempt to answer the question, "Why do I work?"

A prominent American automotive corporation did a survey several years ago and, among other questions, they asked one thousand 45-year-old males, "Why do you work?" The most popular answer to the question was, "Because I have to." This answer suggests two things:

1. Many people work because of the responsibilities they've chosen to fulfill to their loved ones and creditors.

2. These same people may lose sight of their longer-term dreams and goals because of the sometimes-overwhelming short-term responsibilities they choose to accept.

Undefined and unwritten dreams fade away

One example of this is that many young adults today have the largely un-clarified dream of someday achieving some form of financial independence. Still, history and reality suggest without receiving help, very few people are actually going to achieve their financial desire. Less than 5% of Americans actually achieve this status, and we live in a country that provides some of the highest levels of opportunity in the world.

Without some form of written plan to keep us focused on attempting positive headway on the road to financial security it becomes very easy to become entangled in the day-to-day issues, which seem to require so much energy. Over time, we can lose sight of dreams for the future and become frustrated with our lack of progress.

When we produce work focused on only short-term gain we often create for ourselves long-term pain

Many people also desire to work in some role providing them with the opportunity to be interested, challenged and personally satisfied. And yet, the Herman Group's study suggests that over half of Americans are not realizing any level of this desire either.

We need dreams to keep us focused, energetic and directed when many of the issues and requirements at work attempt to tax us beyond what we feel are our reasonable capabilities. There are always so many people pulling at us from every direction. In an attempt to satisfy the needs of everyone around us, the day-to-day work of the job may become even more difficult to enjoy. We may even begin to feel as if no one really cares about us. If we don't keep our dreams fresh and vivid in our minds we can become so focused on the "fray of the day" that we can actually loose sight of the bigger picture that we've envisioned. Ultimately, we may set ourselves up for the long-term pain of never realizing the hopes and dreams that we had for ourselves when we where younger.

Dreams fuel the desire to persevere through hardship

And what about personal hardship? We know you have a life outside of work. As managers, so do we. Another reason our dreams are so important is that we contend with the issues of our personal life as well as the issues of the job. It can all become a little overwhelming and we can easily lose our enthusiasm for a job that many of us hoped would help us to get a leg up on our future opportunities.

We're all more capable than we know

As human beings we have each been given a gift. This gift is an ability to endure much more than we believe possible and achieve much more than we believe ourselves capable. All we need do, in order to begin exploring and realizing our potential, is to employ the mechanisms that enhance our natural abilities.

Consider this observation from Benjamin Franklin:

A life without dreams becomes hardship

There is an old saying that goes like this:

"Whatever we vividly imagine, ardently desire, sincerely believe and enthusiastically act upon must inevitably come to pass."

Anonymous

We believe this to be true.

So, let's get started…

Exercise: Creating My "Dreams" List

Imagine that Time, Money and Support from your friends or family were as abundant as needed... What would you do, have or become?

Instructions:

In the spaces provided create a list of your dreams. (Forget reason. Dare to dream. Let the past become history and envision the future that you'd like to create. *We must live in our imaginations, not in our memories!*)

Examples: Retire at 60, Send my child to the best college, Take a trip around the world, etc...

1. _____

2. _____

3. _____

4. _____

5. _____

6. _____

7. _____

8. _____

Chapter 2

Creating Your Future

How many times have you thought about creating a plan? If you're like many people you've probably thought about creating plans for some specific purpose and you may have even done some planning.

Here is a great reason for planning:

When you don't know where you're going…all roads lead there.

Paraphrased—Lewis Carroll

It's easy to end up lost, or unfulfilled when you lack direction and purpose. Most people seem to have some idea of where their life is heading. Very few actually create written plans for the trip. We all possess the ability to achieve our own happiness, and we should employ the tools that will produce for us the future we have chosen.

We are all moving toward our future. We will go happily and willingly, or we will go kicking and screaming. But, we're all going.

Tomorrow never comes. Some people are waiting on tomorrow. They think, "I'll start my planning…tomorrow. I'll change my attitude…tomorrow." Tomorrow, I'm going to start figuring out what I want and how to get it." Tomorrow never comes.

If we are going to get the most out of the job we have today and the work we do, we must start to evaluate our current position and define what our intentions are for our current and possible future roles with the company.

As your managers, we know some of you are occasionally frustrated with various components of your job. It's O.K. We sometimes get frustrated too. The perspective we prefer to focus on is:

What do I expect to get out of the relationship I have with this company? And, am I getting what I need in order to be happy? If not, what am "I" doing about it?

We believe every employee should routinely ask him or herself these questions. We want you to be happy at work. We want you to feel productive here. The truth is…if you determine what you want and will share that with us, it makes it a lot easier for us to help you obtain it. We have some suggestions and tools that help us managers to get the most out of our job and we'd like to pass those strategies on to you.

Ten Career Enhancement Strategies:

1. Be Aware

Take mental notes. Stay alert and be aware of the people and situations around you. This awareness will provide you with the opportunities that we all need to learn new things that could enhance our situation, career and potential.

2. Learn Something New

Try to learn something new every day. This doesn't mean you have to try to learn a new skill every day. It may be something like a better way to communicate with peers, your supervisor or other departments. It may be as simple as choosing to work each day with a positive attitude and happy disposition.

3. Align Yourself With Your Company

Understand what the company's mission and goals are. Attempt to find ways to contribute to the "big picture." Understanding your role and how it fits into the scheme of things will help you to gain a sense of personal value and take you off of the home team bench by putting you in the game. Ask yourself, "How can I make a difference from my current role or position?" We all know that opportunity is more likely to come to the person who applies him or herself. Figure out what the company wants to accomplish and find a way to participate in that achievement.

4. Look for Your Next Opportunity

By engaging yourself and your job you begin to create opportunity for yourself which, in many cases, would not otherwise occur. It becomes much easier to get engaged and stay engaged when you've identified the next step in your career. The most important question in taking advantage of any opportunity or solving any problem is, "what am I willing to do next?" Engaging yourself helps you to create personal satisfaction and engaging your job helps you to uncover opportunities for your own happiness. We know if you don't get what you need on your current job you may begin to look elsewhere. We'd love to have you continue to work with us!

5. Do the Right Thing

Honesty, trust, integrity and credibility are the cornerstones of all great relationships. Regardless of our role in the company, we all have a responsibility to perform our job function to the very best of our ability. Let people know that you care. Like you, we also care about our clients, the people we work with and the company mission. Doing what is right is always the right thing to do. Consider that everyone eventually leaves the company. How will people remember you? What legacy will you leave behind? Help those that struggle. Be an inspiration to those in need. Always tell the truth and, if you make a promise, do your very best to keep it. Doing these things helps us all to live a life worth living.

6. Be Proactive

Look for ways to improve what you do. No matter what your role with the company, those people who look for ways to make things better commonly find better ways. Those who expect things to worsen commonly find problems as well. Make the choice to proactively participate. You have great value and so does your perspective on our business. Find a way to participate beyond the company's normal expectations for an employee in your role and we promise it won't go unnoticed. We believe your ideas and creativity have merit. Please allow us the opportunity to understand them so we can partner with you to make things better for everyone.

7. Communicate Up

We don't really want to tell you what "to do." We would prefer you make those decisions on your own. Still, we would like to know what "you're doing." So help us. Please communicate up. We may have some special insight, which might help you use your time more effectively. Or we might possess some special knowledge that could make your job a little easier. When employees keep managers informed of plans and outcomes, it helps us to more often work from the "same page." Besides, we want to give you feedback. Communicating up allows us more opportunity to express exactly what we think about the job you're doing and provides a forum for us to thank and recognize your good work.

8. Be Patient with Peers

We know you bond with and appreciate some peers more than others. That's natural. We are all more likely to appreciate those people we like. And yet, everyone has value and the potential to contribute at some level. Be patient with everyone and you may find that someone will actually contribute in an unexpected way. A new employee that knows very little about her new job may bring a level of enthusiasm that has declined in a more tenured player. The more tenured player might use this same enthusiasm to pull himself out of a slump. One the other hand, tenured players may possess certain knowledge about the nuances of a job or a company that newer employees might find useful. This contribution may assist the newer employee in improving productivity or personal satisfaction. Every one around you may, in some way, benefit your growth, development and opportunity on the job. So…be patient with peers! Leverage your time, talent, attitude, skills and abilities with others.

9. Balance Work with Play

We're sure you've heard, "All work and no play makes Jack a dull boy." Work hard. Make a difference. Make improvements and smile while you do these things. Enjoy the time that you have with family and friends. Enjoy hobbies. Get plenty of exercise and eat healthfully. Remember that we don't live to work, we work to live. So live well and balance work with play.

10. Create a Career Map and Review it Regularly

We are all better prepared when we know where it is we want to go. By creating a Career Map that consists of Values, Interests, Attitudes, Competencies and Career Strategy we define our best possible work related situations. By reviewing this map regularly, we keep the vision of our priorities and desires fresh in our minds so we may most easily uncover and identify the best path to our chosen future.

Exercise: Creating My Career Map

Your Career Map should consist of 5 elements. The elements are Values, Interests, Attitudes, Competencies, and Career Strategy.

Instructions:

Answer the questions below to determine your chosen attributes for each of these elements. *(Be honest with yourself. For this exercise, focus on what you think, feel and believe and not how you think others may answer these questions for you. It's your perspective that is important here.)*

1. **Career Values:** Your career values are those things you must personally exhibit or obtain on the job in order to feel satisfied with your work.

Which "Values" are most important to you?

(Circle all that apply and/or add additional important values in the provided blank spaces. Then, stack rank your top 5. Number 1 should be most important to you and number 5 should be least important of your top 5 Values priorities.)

Honesty	Trust	Credibility
Helping Others	Public Contact	Working with a Team
Friendship	Competition	Serving Others
Making Decisions	Having Authority	Working Under Pressure
People Influence	Working Alone	Knowledge
Creativity	Change	Following the Rules
Excitement	Adventure	Independence
Lifestyle	Morality	Free Time
Money	Pride	Being an Expert

_____   _____   _____

2. **Career Interests:** Your career interests are tasks and educational/developmental opportunities that you feel you must be allowed to explore on the job in order to feel satisfied.

What would you like to do on the job that would help you feel more fulfilled? (Make a list of these career interests. Examples: Problem solving, team involvement, customer issues, special projects, mentoring, etc…)

_____	_____
_____	_____
_____	_____

3. **Attitudes:** Your attitude is your chosen state of mind, the way you feel and your resulting behavior.

What attitudes will best serve you and help you get the most out of the relationships you have with your customers, peers, managers and company? (Create a list of these attitudes. Examples: Happy, helpful, trusting, adaptable, open minded, caring, tenacious, etc…)

_____	_____	_____
_____	_____	_____
_____	_____	_____
_____	_____	_____

4. **Competencies:** Your competencies are observable and measurable characteristics, which include—Using Knowledge, Demonstrating Skills, Behaviors and Abilities.

What Competencies do you possess that have helped you or can help you in your work? (Create a list of your Competencies. Examples include: Patience, Attention to detail, Composure, Decision Quality, Compassion, Customer Focus, Ethics and Values, Humor, Problem Solving, etc…)

_____	_____	_____
_____	_____	_____
_____	_____	_____
_____	_____	_____
_____	_____	_____

5. **Career Strategy:** Your career strategy is a loose combination of the first 4 elements to create a "Big Picture" perspective of what you feel you need in order for you to be happy in your work. These elements can be used to help you receive more value in your current role or position. These elements can also be used to help define where you want to be at some future point in your career.

Review the first 4 elements. In the space below, attempt to combine your answers to create your ideal job situation.

Example: It's important to me that I'm allowed to be honest, helpful, an expert, and encouraged to compete with others. I love problem solving, interacting with customers, working on or with technology and learning new things. The attitudes that best help me on the job are honesty, integrity, being positive, creative and adaptable. I get along well with most everyone and I'm good at diagnosing problems, discovering solutions and helping others to understand what needs to be done to eliminate problems in the future. I really like being an engineer and enjoy the people I work with here!

Now it's your turn:

_____

_____

_____

_____

_____

_____

_____

_____

_____

_____

Chapter 3

Planning For Success

Many people want something. Fewer achieve their desired results. There is a formula for achieving results.

Vision + Planning + Competent Effort = Results

Most people have some idea of what they'd like their future to be. We've heard employees say things like, "Someday...I'd like to work on a team where everyone gets along." Or, "Someday...I'd like to do work which excites me." We've even heard, "Someday...I'd like to be a manager."

Well, someday could be closer than you think. We'd like to help you bring the distant horizon in your mind into clear focus and closer to you.

We've gained some valuable knowledge on our journey from employee to manager and we'd like to pass on to you the catalyst that can bring your chosen future closer to you and maybe even into your current reality.

Success doesn't come to you...you go to it!

The first step in creating your own future is "Vision." You've begun developing your vision by working through the "Dreams List" and "Career Map" exercises in this book. There are many people having some level of difficulty seeing their future inside their current company. There's nothing wrong with that if it has always been their intention not to stay. Still, if you would like to achieve higher levels of personal opportunity and satisfaction with your current company, we believe we can help. The exercises you've already completed will help you to envision more happiness and satisfaction from your relationship with your company.

The next step would be to begin to develop a more *Tactical Map*. This map should include a series of steps and tasks you plan to accomplish which will speed you on your way to your desired goals. The Tactical Map has three specific benefits.

Benefit #1:

A one thousand-mile journey begins with a single step.

Chinese Proverb

Quite often people have a general idea of what he or she would like the future to look like, but no clarity of steps, procedures, tasks or work which needs to be produced in order to achieve it. A tactical approach needs to be created to achieve the more expansive and possibly longer "Big Picture." A *Tactical Map* helps you to understand more clearly what actions should be taken in order to logically realize the larger vision you've begun to create for yourself.

Benefit #2:

Motivation is "internal" not "external"

In order to achieve the plans you create for yourself it is extremely important you begin to visualize not only the end result but also the path you must travel to those achievements. Developing, consistently reviewing, visualizing and, if needed, changing your written plans allows you to make better decisions, effectively organize time use and reduce stress.

We've learned over time that "if it's going to be…it's up to me!" We can't count on others to be our motivators. It's nice when it happens, but we are each in charge of our personal motivation. Visualizing and understanding the path in front of you while completing the tasks you've envisioned to produce your chosen results, motivates you to keep pressing onward. But there is an additional value of Tactical Mapping, which shouldn't be overlooked.

Benefit #3:

Anything you think about long enough and hard enough is bound to come true

If you consistently think of good things, you receive good things. If you consistently think of bad things, it's the bad things that manifests in your life.

As we've said, we've learned that we all need, at some level, personal and positive motivation in our lives. The trick is to find those motivators that can be sustained over time and not just "fire you up" and get you started. Too often people come up with great "ideas" only to have the idea and the result fade away over time. You need a mechanism that allows you to stay focused and motivated during your journey. Working with Tactical Maps provides you with the common and consistent motivation that helps you "stay the course" and achieve higher levels of chosen success.

According to the Yerkes-Dodson Law, *(The Relation of Strength of Stimulus to Rapidity of Habit Formation),* too much or too little motivation can actually work against you in achieving your goals. Too much motivation and we tend to burn out too quickly. Too little motivation and we tend to become frustrated while waiting on longer term results. Tactical Mapping provides the appropriate amounts of stimulation and motivation in order to achieve the most profound short and long-term results.

 *Exercise: Tactical Mapping*

Your Tactical Map should consist of 6 important elements:

1.   Creating Goals

2.   Short Range Objectives

3.   Leveraging Strengths

4.   Personal Improvement Strategies

5. Identifying and Overcoming Obstacles

6. Visualization Aids and Commitments

1. **Creating Goals**: Goals should be longer-term objectives. They should also be specific and measurable. Meaning, you should be able to easily assess whether you're getting closer to, or further away from the result you envisioned. Goals should also be important to you and be assigned a date by which you've chosen to accomplish them.

Answer the following questions to create a business or personal goal for yourself.

A. What would you like to accomplish that should take six or more months to achieve?

Example:
"I'm going to be the most productive employee in my department."

_____

_____

B. What benchmarks or milestones will you look for to measure your progress?

Examples:
Increased reward, better customer service ratings, less job stress, etc…

_____

_____

C. How will you be able to tell if you're <u>not</u> getting closer to your goal?

Examples:
Making less money, friction on the team, personal stress, missed deadlines, etc…

_____

_____

D. When specifically would you like to realize/accomplish this goal?
(List the chosen date by which you plan to achieve your goal.)

_____

2. **Short Range Objectives**: Short Range Objectives are those things you must do or accomplish which will take you closer to your goal. These are the tasks you must sometimes accomplish on the road to achievement. The time frame to accomplish these objectives or tasks may range from something you want to do today; up to something you intend to do 3 months from now.

Create a list of Short Range Objectives

(Don't attempt to over think this exercise. Paint with a broad brush. It isn't important you think of every detail. It's only important you come up with what you consider to be the most significant actions for you to begin and reach your goal achievement.)

Examples:
Reviewing my job description, updating my technical knowledge and skills, reviewing and if possible improving my work procedures and process, etc…

1. _____

2. _____

3. _____

3. **Leveraging Strengths**: You have strengths! Everyone does. There are things you do well which will help you in your goal achievement.

What are your strengths and how might you use them to help you reach your goal?

My Strength   How can I use my strength to help achieve my goal?

Example:
I am creative   I will look for and find new ways to better do my job.

_____   _____

_____   _____

_____   _____

4. **Personal Improvement Strategies**: Everyone has at least some room for improvement. Introspection is not always easy, but usually rewarding. You may find improvement opportunities in the areas of Attitudes, Knowledge or Skill.

What are your improvement areas and what will you do to improve?

Improvement Opportunities   What will I do to help me improve in this area?

Example:
Planning   I will create, review, and consistently update my tactical map

_____   _____

_____   _____

_____   _____

5. **Identifying and Overcoming Obstacles**: As we attempt to accomplish things that are important to us, obstacles sometimes get in the way. We should try to proactively identify these obstacles and begin to create a plan or strategy to avoid or overcome them.

Possible Obstacles   Plans to Overcome the Obstacle

Example:
Job stress   Review my plans and celebrate small successes

_____   _____

_____   _____

_____   _____

6. **Visualization Aids and Commitments**: Visualization Aids are things you use to help you Visualize the goal you've created for yourself and the actions you will take along the way to your achievement. People who have experienced the true power of goal setting know that the more often you visualize your goals the more likely you are to achieve them!

Here's how it works! Your brain is a very special tool. It has the ability to attach the picture you create of your future to the consequences and/or benefits of that future along with the emotions you'll likely experience once you've achieved it. In effect, you can overcome time and space and create for yourself *"memories of the future."* This can be a tremendous motivator when times get tough and it also allows you to actually enjoy the emotional benefit of an achievement long before it's actually realized. The more often you visualize your goal the stronger and more motivating it will become! Haven't you ever looked forward to something like a vacation? You can become very exited about things we haven't even done yet! You think about where we are going, whom you'll be with and what you'll be doing. You anticipate the enjoyment you expect to get while you're on the vacation. You work with pleasure to complete the tasks that must be accomplished so your vacation can begin and go smoothly. It's almost like being there...before you get there! Visualization helps you to stay motivated while you progress toward goal attainment.

What will you use to visualize your future achievements and how often will you do it?

Visualization Aid

Example:
My written plans, smiling happy customers, employee of the month award, etc...

1. _____

2. _____

3. _____

4. _____

5. _____

How often will you visualize?

_____

What are the likely benefits of your regular visualizations?

_____

As your managers, we hope you will be willing to share with us the Tactical Maps and plans you've created for yourself so we might assist you in some way and share in the joy of your achievements. We look forward to having you bring your chosen future to our attention.

From all of us…Thank you!

Chapter 4

The Value of Position Descriptions

As mentioned before, we have more in common than you might think. Another of those commonalities is we all depend on our work to provide an important source of income to support our families and ourselves in a lifestyle we feel is reasonable. Our current job also serves as the vehicle we expect to carry us into an even more rewarding business and financial future.

Good work today…fuels tomorrow

Most of us work to earn the money needed to take care of our current financial obligations and hopefully pay for any future needs we may uncover. You may also hope that your current position will help to propel you towards some future opportunity with your company. The challenge is that unless you can perform your current role and responsibilities to everyone's reasonable satisfaction, none of your income needs or future opportunities is likely to be realized. In other words, if you can't successfully perform the duties of the job you have now, your future dreams and goals begin to run out of fuel.

Conflict is the mother of disaster

Whenever there is conflict on the job, everyone's work and life becomes more difficult. Even the simplest task can become arduous when things aren't running smoothly and responsibilities are not being fulfilled. Have you ever felt like no one at work was on the "same page?" Have you ever wondered why someone doesn't create some guidelines to help you secure the outcomes you'd like to accomplish on the job? Do you ever ponder why someone doesn't synchronize the team's functions, align you more closely with the team vision and provide you the opportunity to clarify the expected results with your manager? Well, in most companies there are such written guidelines. It's called a "Position Description." This document has also been referred to as a Job Description.

The more detailed the map…the easier the journey

Plainly put, the position description provides us with the details of our work responsibility and the expectations our company has of us. When we managers provide you with a position description, we do so in order to help you understand what specific behaviors and work should be exhibited and accomplished for you to be most successful, productive and happy in your job. Actually, a position description has several important functions and benefits.

Position Description functions and benefits:

1. It provides managers and employees a common understanding of work expectations.

2. It lists the tasks and behaviors that best promote the results an employee needs to produce on the job.

3. It lists the specific competencies that, when exhibited and enhanced, propel an employee to the next level of opportunity and/or responsibility.

4. It creates an opportunity for managers to help employees achieve greater levels of productivity with less stress, more success and more abundant future possibilities.

Future opportunity is created by current success

Whatever you want from the relationship you have with your current employer, it is safe to say that those things can only be logically realized when you become proficient in your current role or position. You must create opportunity by building on hard work and job success. Only after you begin to focus on your own improvement in our current job do the doors of future opportunity open to you.

Your first step in creating more opportunity at work is to clearly define and recognize why you might choose to do the work of your current job.

 *Exercise: Why do I work?*

We managers believe it is important for every employee to identify the reasons and motivations that compel him or her to work. These motivators can vary for different employees and yet some may be more common. It's not our intention to tell you what is supposed to be important to you; we would like you to decide for yourself. We don't believe that we can necessarily find your motivations for you, but we do believe we can help you activate the motivations you uncover.

We all work. We work for many reasons. Defining and understanding those reasons can provide each of us the enthusiasm we need to get us through the difficult days and all of the energy we'll need to take best advantage of any opportunity that may present itself to us.

Instructions:

In the space provided, create a list of your specific reasons and motivations for working. (Think who, what and why.)

(If you happen to think of more than 10, feel free to write any additional reasons and motivations as well.)

Examples:

My family, my retirement, financial independence, a new house, etc…

1. _____   6. _____

2. _____   7. _____

3. _____   8. _____

4. _____   9. _____

5. _____   10. _____

The good work we produce every day provides each of us with the opportunity to realize the motivation and desired outcomes that inspire us to return to work. In other words, these are our reasons for working.

Just like in life, work consists of good days and difficult days.

Challenge is inevitable…winning is an option

Everyone faces challenge on the job. We face challenges and know you do too. Some days are better than other days. One good work objective is to get into the best possible position to overcome these struggles and achieve a desirable result with the least amount of stress and confusion.

By continuing to define and focus on the reasons why you choose to work, it can compel you to remain more positive in moments of difficulty and promotes resourcefulness when overcoming challenge.

Also, there is a way to proactively eliminate certain challenges on the job and make the largest number of personal opportunities available. The key is to understand, focus on and improve your level of competence in your current role or position. The tool that will best serve you in this endeavor is a Position Description.

Exercise: Reviewing My Position Description

Everyone who works can benefit from occasionally reviewing his or her position description. By doing so, you better understand what you need to do each day to become most successful in your

job. You can also identify areas of possible improvement. Once these areas have been identified and improvement has been made, your work becomes more enjoyable and productive.

As your managers, we would relish the opportunity to help you simplify your life at work and achieve higher levels of satisfaction. By reviewing your position description, you may be able to help us help you. Please consider coming to us and letting us know which improvement areas you're currently focused on and allow us the opportunity to help you. We're not saying that we're experts or we're smarter than you are. We're saying that we care about you and we'd like to help…if you'll allow us to.

Instructions:

Locate a copy of your Position Description. Review each of the activities or behaviors listed in your Position Description and answer these two questions:

1. **On a scale from 1-5 (1=low 5=high), how important is this task or behavior to successfully achieving the expectations that the company has for me?** (As you review each item consider the impact on the productivity and results the company expects if you don't perform this task or behavior. Then consider what positive benefits can be achieved if you perform it to the very best of your ability.)

2. **On a scale from 1-5 (1=low 5=high), how important is this task or behavior in helping me get what I want out of my relationship with my current company?** (As you review each item consider the impact on your personal goal achievement if you don't perform this task or behavior. Then consider what positive benefits can be achieved if you perform it to the very best of your ability.)

As you determine your ratings for both questions, write down your ratings next to each item on your position description.

Now, go back and review your rating of each item on your Position Description. What conclusions can you draw from this exercise?

Example:

"Even though I perform most of my job responsibilities well there are a few tasks I tend to avoid or maybe not do at all. These are process paperwork, event planning and returning customer complaint calls."

_____

_____

_____

_____

_____

_____

Please consider sharing with us your conclusions. We value your opinions and if by chance there is something we can do to help you, we would like to know. We know it may sometimes appear we ask you to perform tasks that have little meaning. But, the truth is, every expectation written in a position description has some level of value to you, the company, the team and/or the customer.

So, as a result of this exercise what actions might you consider taking to best serve your own goals and the goals of other employees in your company?

What should you consider doing differently going forward?

Example:

"I will schedule time each day to complete paperwork, review needed plans and return every customer's call."

_____

_____

_____

_____

Chapter 5

Winning Behavior

We live and work in a world where we are all, at least to some extent, co-dependent.

Everything of value we will ever accomplish, will in some way… involve other people

In many ways a company is very much like a community. Regardless of our department we are dependent on others to perform their functions and responsibilities so our work may have true substance and value. The relationships we have with our co-workers, managers, and other departments can either enhance our opportunity for achievement and happiness on the job or hinder it. Many of us may actually spend more time with the people with whom we work with than we do with our own families. And yet in some cases, these work relationships are strained. This commonly occurs because of someone's inappropriate or *un-adult like* behavior.

Indifference kills relationships

Whenever an employee disregards the feelings or needs of his or her co-workers, the almost inevitable outcome will be relationship tension. If that tension is allowed to exist too long without being addressed or repaired the result can be a strained or broken relationship. There are many reasons for this occurrence in the workplace. We believe the most common catalyst for this irritable tension between co-workers is caused when someone doesn't possess a broad enough understanding or concern of how personal actions and behaviors impact other people. If this condition exists in any employee, that person may feel it's less important to consider the possible impact on others before taking action.

A common example of this in the workplace is when an employee makes a decision selfishly. If an employee makes a decision without considering the impact it may have on co-workers, chances are someone's job is likely to become more difficult. This can cause frustration for the effected department's employees and substantial friction in the relationship gears.

I am responsible for 50% of all my relationships

We all have a responsibility to conduct ourselves in a professional and adult manner when interacting with other people. Every relationship in the world requires both parties to exhibit a reasonable amount of compassion, effort and communication if the relationship is going to endure and thrive.

I am responsible for 100% of my behavior

No one can make you do anything. As managers, we've learned that we may have the ability to influence you, when you allow it, but any action you take is always your choice. No one can make you happy or sad. You choose those emotions for yourself. We're not suggesting when bad things happen it doesn't impact you. What we're suggesting is your attitude and the behavior you exhibit as a result of that attitude is your choice. If you are compelled to interact with others you should also feel compelled to exhibit reasonable and appropriate behavior. You should exhibit behavior that will improve relationships, strengthen everyone's chances for success and enhance your life and the lives of the people around you so everyone can be happier, more productive and less stressed.

What is the impact on you when someone acts without regard to the implications that action may have on you and your attitude or your work? We know it can be frustrating and can even become somewhat painful over time.

There are many benefits realized when everyone always chooses to act like an adult.

The respect of others is earned by our behaviors

Treat other people with respect and watch how quickly they respect you in return. This really isn't a secret, but it has sometimes appeared to be less than common knowledge in the workplace. Can you think of an example when someone wasn't acting the way you felt he or she should? Everyone has their own agenda and rightfully so. We are all responsible for and focused on our own needs. Still, when the employees and managers of any company realize the true value of working in harmony to perform a service in the marketplace, they obtain a much quicker and more potent acquisition of their own goals. In addition, everyone is happier and more satisfied on the job. When this harmony is achieved, it is always more of a win-win situation.

If everyone behaves like an adult does it make a positive difference? Yes! We all know adult behavior makes a positive difference in the workplace. The important question is "How do we get everyone to act like adults all of the time?"

Change the way you think and act toward others and watch how quickly they change the way they think and act toward you.

James Allen (Paraphrased)

We can't make other people change, but we can influence them over time with our own consistent, appropriate behavior. We managers recognize most employees exhibit good behavior most of the time. And yet it's the more rare occasion of inappropriate behavior that seems to cause many of the problems and much of the "tell-tale" conversation at work. Maybe if we all work together we could completely eliminate the unproductive behaviors from our workplace. When everyone works together to make the workplace a more enjoyable and adult like environment…everyone wins.

Over time, we've been able to identify and document the most important adult or what we call "MVP" Behaviors exhibited by professionals on the job today. These 13 behaviors are separated into categories that make up the four cornerstones of what is commonly called "Business Maturity."

The four categories of Business Maturity are:

1. **Headset** (General mindset or attitude)
2. **Adaptability** (Ability to transition effectively through change)
3. **Self Sufficiency** (Desire and ability to work independently)
4. **Job Effectiveness** (Ability to perform responsibly the work of the job)

Each of these four categories represents an important component of Business Maturity. Once these MVP Behaviors become the focus of and implemented by any employee, his or her work becomes easier to produce, there is more harmony with peers and work becomes a more enjoyable experience.

These are the 13 suggested MVP Behaviors combined with the meaning and intent of each:

Headset:

1. **Criticizes Privately/Compliments Publicly**
   This person understands appropriate channeling and will offer complaints to his/her supervisor only. The individual is mindful of others and their feelings.

2. **Exhibits the Appropriate Degree of Humility**
   This individual shows consistent discipline to control his/her ego in all situations. Confidence is not arrogance that distorts his/her true skills.

3. **Supports Teamwork by Helping Others**
   The person contributes to team goals, is available and willing to help peers and participates fully in work related team activities.

Adaptability:

1. **Actively Seeks Better Ways**
   This person maintains sensible flexibility and remains open to change. His/her focus is on continuous improvement.

2. **Learns Quickly**
   The person accepts responsibility for his/her own improvement and exhibits appropriate levels of determination and zeal in improvement situations.

3. **Supports Others in Their Attempts to Deal with Change**
   The individual understands the emotions of others in improvement situations and supports/assists their efforts as they transition through change.

Self Sufficiency:

1. **Attempts to Solve Problems Before Seeking Help**
   The individual works to find solutions on his/her own versus relying solely on others for answers. He contributes ideas and enjoys problem solving.

2. **Proactively Grows Skills and Knowledge**
   This person feeds on new experiences and building his/her knowledge and expertise. She seeks information and immerses herself in learning opportunities.

3. **Displays Initiative**
   The person possesses the inner desire and commitment to move his/her performance forward. He takes appropriate pride in his contributions, and is always looking to make improvements.

Job Effectiveness:

1. **Develops a Network of Resources**
   The person understands the value of leveraged resources and tenaciously works to broaden his/her frequently accessed information and support mechanisms.

2. **Avoids Procrastination**
   This person pursues goals, improvement, opportunity and achievement. He/she is not afraid to step up and out. He seeks success and is willing to attempt what others are not.

3. **Attentive to Details/Highly Organized**
   The person's work effort is disciplined and consistent. He/she desires achievement without confusion or mistakes.

4. **Highly Developed Job Related Skills**
   The individual shows consistent discipline to learn and build his/her competence and confidence. He performs job tasks with ease and precision.

Consider the job related employee issues that could be proactively averted if all employees would simply follow these easy to understand rules of MVP Behavior. If these behaviors become the standard for all members of any company, everyone experiences more peace of mind, more productivity on the job, fewer issues of conflict and the whole organization can become a more cohesive elite, high performance team.

Wouldn't that be a great place to work!

Exercise: Rating MVP Behaviors

We managers believe the consistent demonstration of MVP Behaviors from all employees can improve satisfaction and productivity for everyone at work. We recognize that most people do the right things most of the time. Still, everyone may have some room for improvement. What a wonderful world it could be if everyone would do his or her level best to always exhibit these behaviors. Please, always demonstrate the best possible example for those who look up to and believe in you. Thank you!

Instructions:

Using the provided rating system, rate yourself in each of the MVP Behaviors. 1 = Poor, 5 = Excellent (If needed, refer to the previously provided explanations for each behavior.)

MVP Employee Behaviors	Rating
Criticized privately/compliments publicly	1 2 3 4 5
Exhibits the appropriate degree of humility	1 2 3 4 5
Supports teamwork by helping others	1 2 3 4 5
Actively seeks better ways	1 2 3 4 5
Learns quickly	1 2 3 4 5
Supports others in their attempt to deal with change	1 2 3 4 5
Attempts to solve problems before seeking help	1 2 3 4 5
Proactively grows skills and knowledge	1 2 3 4 5

Displays initiative	1	2	3	4	5
Develops a network of resources	1	2	3	4	5
Avoids procrastination	1	2	3	4	5
Attentive to details/highly organized	1	2	3	4	5
Highly developed job related skills	1	2	3	4	5

Which two areas might offer you the best opportunity for personal improvement going forward?

Behavior #1: _____

Behavior #2: _____

Please consider sharing your chosen improvement behaviors with us so we might provide you with the support and recognition you so richly deserve.

Thank you!

Chapter 6

The Greatest Gift

This is one of the basic "truths" of life:

The only real improvement is "self improvement"

No matter how badly someone else may want you to improve, if you don't choose improvement for yourself, it won't happen. Wouldn't you agree it would be nice if we could make other people change? As an example, when a co-worker neglects to do something you feel he or she should have done and it causes more work for you. You might wish you could make them change. You might even bring the situation to us hoping, as managers, we can make him or her change. Alas, we really can't *make* your co-worker change either. Even when we attempt to hold your co-worker or you accountable, changing is a personal choice.

Don't misunderstand. We always hope every new employee will become successful in our company. We often use the latest technologies to hire new employees who have the highest probability of success. More times than not though, an employee's success on the job comes down to the attitude, desire and tenacity the employee is willing to commit to work, the team and his or her personal commitment to change and improve.

No one can make those unwilling to change or improve do so. We must all decide for ourselves to make the best use of the tools and leadership our company provides. We would like to help good employees like you continue to improve so you may take best advantage of any opportunity our company might provide for you.

We believe in the first rule of self-esteem:

Whatever you fill your mind with, and focus yourself on, is what you become

Employees who attempt to just "get by" often find themselves being passed over for opportunities at work. People who live their lives satisfied to maintain the "status quo" commonly improve slowly, if at all, and may find they struggle at work just to keep up. Those who attempt to do very little at work tend to receive little in return. People, who focus only on problems at work and never solutions, tend to endure more problems. And, people who convince themselves they are unhappy and have no opportunity on the job usually find out they are right.

What these things suggest to us is this…

Anything you think about long enough and hard enough is bound to come true

If you focus on good, you receive more good. If you focus on the bad, you receive more bad. And if you focus on nothing, you receive what someone else wants to give you, good or bad.

We have all been given a tremendous gift. The ability of personal improvement! We have been granted all of the tools we need to become even better than we are now. You don't have to go out and buy these tools. They come as part of your basic programming. It's in you DNA. You're adaptable. You change. You improve. You're a winner! And most importantly…we believe in you!

Success is more a result of attitude than aptitude

We've all seen employees with little or no formal education become extremely successful. We've witnessed people that no one gave a chance to succeed over-come huge obstacles in order to do so. What makes the difference between long-term success and failure? The answer is, it all starts with the right attitude. Why is the right attitude so important? That's easy, because everything around us is changing. As the world changes so do customers. As customers change so do companies. And as companies' change…we must also change. We must improve. We must endure the hardships of improvement in order to achieve the rewards of success. Everyone struggles at one time or another at work. It's normal. It's expected. It's part of living, and it's part of growing.

Improvement is the greatest gift we can give to ourselves

Please understand if we could, we would make improvements for you. We sometimes lie awake at night attempting to devise ways to make your improvement transitions as easy as possible. We have meetings. We provide training. We try to make learning and improving fun. But the truth is, improvement is something you can only do for yourself.

We understand the road to improvement can be littered with hazards. Hazards like quota or productivity expectations. On some days even we wish we could all just stop working and say, "I know. Let's not worry about work today! Let's focus only on personal improvement!" Unfortunately, we can't just stop the work. We must all continue to serve while we also continue toward our own improvement. But, we will make you three promises:

<u>Management Promises:</u>
1. If you'll focus on your improvement we'll do our best to recognize the effort you exert and the improvement in you. In fact, we'll try to help you improve…if you'll ask or allow us to.
2. The more you improve the easier the work becomes.
3. The more you improve the happier you'll become with yourself.

So how do you achieve improvement? By first remembering this:

Success is a road always under construction

At one time or another most people have decided to make some kind of improvement. Whether it was a New Year's resolution, a diet or a work related goal of some kind, everyone considers making improvement. What most people fail to realize is we didn't get the way we are over night. We got the way we are "over time!" If you are intent on personal improvement of any kind, you must first recognize it's most likely going to take a long-term commitment, consistent focus and patience with yourself.

If you choose to strive for personal improvement, there is something we can offer you that will help. We've learned there are 4 steps to self-improvement.

Four Self Improvement Steps:

1. <u>Decide what you want to improve and know why.</u>

   If any personal improvement attempt is going to be successful you must determine what you "specifically" want to improve and why it's important to you to do so. It might help to review some of your determined motivations. You might refer back to your "Dreams List" or your short-term objectives and the longer-term goals you have previously created. These things may provide you the motivation you need for improvement and may also help you to discern specifically what improvements you should consider.

2. <u>Create an improvement plan.</u>

   Write your improvement goals down. Start to create a list of things you'd like to improve and the tasks you'll need to accomplish in order to do so. Visualize these improvements and the benefits you will receive once you have accomplished them.

3. <u>Involve other people.</u>

   Allowing others to share in your goals and desires for improvement helps you to begin creating a support system. We all need help from time to time. Help with motivation. Help with application. Help to remain consistently focused on our objectives. We'd love to be one of the support mechanisms you employ. Our success is tied to your success. More importantly, we care about each one of you. Please consider allowing us to become part of your improvement support group.

4. <u>Celebrate "small" successes.</u>

   Enjoy each moment of the improvement journey. Don't wait to celebrate only after the final objective has been reached. Understand that most real improvement takes time and you're actually making headway every day you continue to work toward your improvement goals. First ask yourself this question. "What will be happening on the road to my improvement objectives?" Make note of those benchmarks and then celebrate and enjoy the incremental success that creates the road to improvement. Most of all, please remember you should be patient with yourself during improvement. Rome wasn't built in a day and life is a journey. Enjoy the trip. We have great confidence in your abilities and would appreciate sharing in your improvement successes with you.

Exercise: Embracing Improvement

Consistent improvement can sometimes feel like more work. And yet, the more you improve the better you feel about yourself and the easier your work becomes. When you choose to focus on continuous improvement, your abilities and opportunities for success are greatly enhanced.

Instructions:

In the space below, identify some possible areas of improvement to embrace. These could be areas of personal study, personal development and/or relationship development. Then list the benefits that you might realize as a result of your improvements. (You may consider referring back to the previous exercises of "Reviewing Your Position Description" and "Rating MVP Behaviors" for inspiration.)

<u>Possible Improvement Areas</u>   <u>Benefits of Improvement</u>

1. _____   _____

     _____

2. _____   _____

     _____

3. _____   _____

     _____

4. _____   _____

Once you have completed the first part of this exercise, review your possible improvement areas and stack rank them in order of importance to you. 1 = Most Important, 4 = Least Important

We recommend that after you have completed this exercise, you consider embracing these improvements at the rate of <u>one per month</u>. Remember, you didn't get the way you are over night. You got the way you are over time. If you are going to make improvements in yourself, you should be patient and understanding. Be patient with yourself and allow time for new behaviors and skills to solidify in your daily activities.

Please believe that we know how difficult it can be to make behavioral or skill improvements and we will appreciate your consistent dedication and effort, even if it takes time to implement the improvements.

We're on your side!

What improvement area have you chosen to begin embracing first and what will you do to achieve this personal improvement?

_____

_____

_____

_____

_____

With whom will you share your improvement goals?

_____   _____

_____   _____

What benchmarks will you celebrate along the way to your improvement?

_____   _____

_____   _____

Chapter 7

Successful Leveraging

In a world where expectations for performance continue to increase, this statement contains genuine value:

The easiest way to be successful in the future is...together

Almost everything of value any person may accomplish in life involves, at some level, other people. Depending on the area of life you've chosen to improve, achieving success may indeed include family, friends, co-workers or even us...your managers. Whenever two or more people work together to achieve a common goal we call that _leveraging_.

The joy of success can actually be diminished when we don't allow others to participate and help us. Why? Because we have no one with whom to truly share the joy. As human beings our sense of accomplishment actually grows stronger when we know other people who care about us have witnessed the hard earned improvement or success. Plus, they in turn experience pleasure because in some small way they helped us to achieve our goals. Because they care about us they actually derive a certain amount of satisfaction from our successes.

A load is more easily moved when everyone pulls in the same direction

As managers we ask all employees to accept personal responsibility for the work that they produce. We believe without the personal commitment from each employee to his or her job, higher levels of productivity may never be reached. What you may be unaware of is, we don't expect you to travel this road to greater productivity and achievement alone. We'd like to help.

We win or lose…together

Our success is tied to your success! So it's actually in our best interest to help you with your career. We are aware that sometimes you might feel a little uncomfortable sharing with the boss what you might feel are your shortcomings. But what we'd like you to understand is we have shortcomings too. We'd like you to know we often reach out to peers, other departments, friends and even our own supervisors for assistance because we've learned goals are frequently more easily accomplished with a little help. If there is a challenge in attaining true and effective leveraging, it may arise because everyone isn't focused on common goals or working in the same direction.

If you reach out for assistance and meet with resistance, it could be the person you're asking doesn't realize the same value you do in your request. You see, he or she may be focused on his or her own needs, objectives or plans.

Teamwork creates momentum for success

If we all work together the likelihood of mutual success and the achievement of our personal and business objectives becomes more probable. This concept, when combined with the value of forging stronger interpersonal relationships on the job, puts us all in a much more likely position to obtain greater satisfaction, and achievement. These accomplishments generally occur with less stress and offer more genuine value to others. You never know. You may be the missing link someone around you is looking for to best serve his or her own initiatives and without you he or she may struggle and fail.

Mutual commitment is the bond that binds effective teams

We understand how easy it is to become singularly focused on the task of the moment or the challenge of the day. We too sometimes find ourselves engrossed in our own needs, difficulties and desires. It's human to be concerned about yourself and those closest to you first. And yet, it's only when you step outside yourself and allow your efforts to be combined with the efforts of others that you begin to achieve greater results. Like the many individual strands of a rope, which pull the weight of burden more easily, or the fingers that work in cooperation and harmony with the hand to grasp any object, so the team works best together to accomplish any goal.

TEAM: Together Everyone Achieves More

"Unknown"

Our ability to work more closely with you to obtain our mutual successes can be enhanced by you. We believe you have great potential and yet many who have possessed potential have fallen short of their capability because they chose to stand-alone. Should you desire to simplify your life rather than complicate it we can offer assistance. When you choose the support of management and the team and then in kind offer your support to others, you begin to realize the power of leveraging very quickly.

Synergy: (definition—The combined sum is greater than it's parts.)

When two or more things, people or organizations work together the result is often greater than the sum of their individual effects or capabilities. This is synergy.

This concept should inspire us all to work together in order to achieve a common good. The common good can be the mutual commitment to and the achievement of individual, team, interdepartmental and company objectives. One of the consistent by-products of retaining this type of mutual commitment is a more productive, happy and fulfilling work environment.

The bottom line is, your job actually gets easier when you help others and allow others to help you!

 *Exercise: Leveraging For Success*

When you, managers and other departments work together, greater achievement is realized with less work, less stress and greater fulfillment. As managers, we would like to commit our time and energy to you in order to help you obtain whatever you desire from your relationship with the company. Our objective is

to simplify and improve your life on the job, not to complicate it. You can best serve yourself by helping others and allowing others to in turn help you. Remember, together everyone achieves more.

Instructions:

Review the lists of expectations below and in the first column on a scale of 1-5, rate the degree of importance for each expectation.

(1 = low importance, 5 = high importance) (As you review each expectation, consider your "big picture." If the expectation is realized does it help or hinder you in the achievement of your own dreams, goals and objectives?)

Next, in the second column determine whether your ability to achieve the expectation might be improved with the help of your manager or supervisor. (Answer either = Yes or No) (As you review each item ask yourself, "Would this be more easily accomplished on my own or with the help of my manager/supervisor?")

Company Expectations	**Rating (1-5)**	**Leverage w/Mgr. (Yes or No)**
Understand & Support Company Decisions		
Work for Company Profitability		
Require Limited Supervision		
Work well with Other Departments		
Exercise Initiative		
Present Requests with a Positive Attitude		
Show Appreciation for Others' Work		
Avoid Reactive Decision Making		
Meets All Deadlines		
Communicate Needs in Advance		

Team Expectations	**Rating** **(1-5)**	**Leverage w/Mgr.** **(Yes or No)**
Exhibit the Appropriate Degree of Humility		
Support Teamwork by Helping Others		
Support Others During Change		
Help Others to Improve		
Complain Only to Your Supervisor		
Maintain a Positive Disposition		
Willing to Share Successes		
Willing to Work With Others		

Customer Expectations	**Rating** **(1-5)**	**Leverage w/Mgr.** **(Yes or No)**
Display Honesty, Trust & Credibility		
Keep Promises and Commitments		
Be an Expert in Your Field		
When You Don't Know, Say So		
Solve all Problems in a Timely Manner		
Answer all Questions in a Timely Manner		
Treat Customers with Respect		
Make Customers Feel Important		
Make Customer Service a Priority		

As a result of this exercise, what actions, commitments or changes are you willing to make?

_____

_____

_____

_____

_____

_____

_____

_____

When will you make these changes and what are the possible benefits to you if you change?

Change: Date: Benefits:

_____   _____   _____

_____   _____   _____

_____   _____   _____

_____   _____   _____

Please feel free to talk to others and us about your chosen changes. The more we support and help each other, the more likely we all benefit. Besides, maybe your commitment to improvement will be the spark someone else needs to light his or her passion for personal change as well.

Chapter 8

Mutual Commitments

It has been said, "As much as some things change, other things stay the same." Here is a concept that has remained true over time:

The most important stride toward success is a commitment to personal excellence

Any person who wishes to achieve more than they already have must consider devoting a certain amount of time to introspection and self-improvement. Introspection is the most powerful, positive and personal developmental tool we possess as human beings and yet, we sometimes don't use it when we could or should. Why? It could be we're concerned about what we might see if we look too closely at the man or woman in the mirror. It could also be we're so very busy running to and from the next activity or task in our attempt to tread water in the waves of ever-increasing expectation.

The fact remains; if we are ever going to achieve the potential of our talent and capability then we must also yearn for improvement.

"Lord, grant that I might always desire more than I can accomplish."

Michelangelo

Most people of great accomplishment have possessed an almost overwhelming desire to improve. We're not suggesting you must envision a "life long" relationship with your current company. Obviously, whether you choose to stay or leave is up to you. But, as long as we're all here, and our dream attainment is closely tied to our ability to work and fund our future, we believe there is tremendous merit in striving to become our very best at we do.

"A man can alter his life by altering his thinking."

William James

We discussed in *Chapter 6, "The Greatest Gift"* the four self-improvement steps. Here are 3 mindsets that can also help you on your road to improvement.

1. <u>Improvement success always begins with a productive attitude.</u>

   Notice we didn't say improvement success always begins with a "positive" attitude. Two primary catalysts, pain and gain, motivate people. Sometimes things go our way. Sometimes things don't. The trick is to remain aware of the controls and influences in our lives so we can determine which might be our most productive attitude. We should employ the attitude that helps us to be most productive in our current situation. As an example, several customer complaints about the same issue might be an indication a company should consider some sort of change. Sure, at the moment you're handling the customer issue it may be an uncomfortable situation. Being uncomfortable may feel a little negative. But, if the situation hadn't come to light neither you nor the company would have recognized the need to change until it was possibly too late to make a positive difference. We must engage both challenge and opportunity as the motivators for improvement.

2. <u>Stretch what you believe are your limits.</u>

   The "Japanese Carp" which is more properly known as a "Koi" is a colorful fish often found in the swirling pools of Japanese gardens and restaurants. The amazing thing about these Koi is if you were to take one after birth and keep it for it's whole life in a small fish bowl, it will never grow any bigger than a large gold fish. Yet, if you put it in a larger pond like the ones you see in some restaurants it will grow to between ten and eighteen inches. If you release it into a lake, this miraculous creature will grow to more than three feet in length.

   The same is true for people. If we create for ourselves "glass ceilings," we will most likely never grow beyond our pre-determined abilities. If we aren't careful, our potential growth can be stunted by our self-imposed limits. We must think big and stretch our limits to create the opportunities of which we are personally capable.

3. <u>Be willing to take some course of action!</u>

> Many people momentarily envision what their life might be like if they would simply do something differently. Still, a large number of people succumb to their self-imposed realities of fear, anxiety or a simple lack of confidence. What they don't seem to understand is if they would simply "start" moving forward and continue to move forward even a little every day, eventually they would most likely overcome these negative thoughts and boundaries.

> Henry David Thoreau said, *"If one advances confidently in the direction of his dreams and endeavors to live the life which he has imagined, he will meet with a success unexpected in common hours."*

After you determine your need for improvement in anything, you must take some productive steps in the appropriate direction. The more you move, the more likely you will achieve. The more you achieve, the more you believe you are capable of even greater things!

We must choose the challenges of achievement or the challenges of getting by

Life is challenge. Either you choose the challenges of achievement and motivate yourself toward continuous improvement, or you choose the challenges of getting by. If you choose the challenges of getting by, you'll most likely find yourself dealing with the same issues today you dealt with yesterday as well as the even greater issues of a depreciating lifestyle. Logically the decision to not improve may not make sense, and still, we all know employees who do seem to choose the hardships of just getting by.

You may be somewhat "comfortable" with the way you are now and you may be willing to deal with repetitive issues or struggles on the job. You may prefer the pain you "do" know, (reoccurring problems), to the pain you "don't" know, (the cost of improvement.) Beginning a journey to improvement may cause uncertainty about the changes or challenges that might be around the next corner because you've never been down that particular road before. To complicate matters even more, you may also become very comfortable with your current condition. Even though you know some improvement would be useful, you might even find yourself saying, "Well, that's just the way things are!"

As your managers, we'd like to politely dispute that idea. We believe that things are the way they are until someone or something changes! We have great confidence in your potential. We believe that together we can make things better for you on the job. We believe you have the ability to improve your situation on the job and in your life. We hope you'll choose the challenges of achievement. We hope you'll choose improvement!

By helping others, we help ourselves

By either choice or default all employees are responsible for and have influence with each other. If you never attempt to improve at work it can impact the coworkers you may interact with during the day. On the other hand, if you focus on your continuous improvement you will also be some level of positive influence for other employees in the environment.

Managers can also be either positive or negative influences. A manager who doesn't care about his or her employees will simply allow them to make it or not on their own. But a manager who does care about the people in their charge will do everything in his or her power to instill in the employees a desire for improvement. We promise to be a caring, helpful manager and to provide the guidance you need to succeed.

By helping you we also help ourselves. Please allow us the opportunity to show you how much faith we have in you and how committed we are to your success.

 ## Exercise: Developing Mutual Commitments

By focusing our attention and efforts on continuous improvement in our work we enhance our abilities and opportunities. When we accept responsibility for improving our own condition we begin to travel the best possible road to success. This road does not need to be traveled alone. As your managers, we hope you will allow us to aid you in your endeavor for improvement.

We have tremendous faith in you, your abilities and your potential. Please allow us to assist you in your improvement journey.

Instructions:

Step 1: Locate a copy of your Position Description. (You may already have the copy you used in *Chapter 4* in *" The Value of Position Descriptions" exercise.*)

Alternatively, you may also ask your manager if he or she has a "Mutual Commitment for Improved Performance" document you might use for this exercise. (This document is used by many managers and is a condensed version of the Position Description and contains an attached rating system.)

Step 2: Once you've located the document you intend to use for this exercise then, review each item of work responsibility listed and on a scale of 1–5 rate your performance. (1 = Poor, 5 = Excellent)

Step 3: Based on your assessment of your abilities, what 3 (Three) or 4 (Four) areas of responsibility or task offer you the best opportunities to improve? (Consider improvement opportunities that will simplify your life, help you to achieve more and reduce any current work related stresses.)

Improvement Opportunity Focus Areas:

_____   _____

_____   _____

Step 4: Consider asking your manager to go through this exercise alone and rate you in each of the areas you've rated yourself. Then meet with your manager to compare notes. Jointly identify 2 or 3 possible areas of improvement focus and together create an improvement action plan.

What areas of focus and improvement did you and your manager agree on and what will be your next steps?

1. _____

_____

_____

2. _____

_____

_____

3. _____

_____

_____

Chapter 9

Developing Resources

At work, where change continues to be our greatest asset and most unyielding foe, this statement means more today than ever:

A smart man isn't one who knows all of the answers...A smart man is one who knows where to look for the answers.

Certainly, we all have a responsibility to become experts in our work and/or field. And yet, with everything changing so dramatically and quickly it is sometimes impossible to know everything about everything on the job. In some work groups the manager has become the primary resource used by employees to answer questions and solve problems. Unfortunately, when this occurs, this answer providing manager may unintentionally limit the amount of versatility, growth and satisfaction his or her employees derive from the work environment.

You can actually become happier, more productive and feel less stress when you develop a wide variety of resources, which offer answers to questions, provide assistance during challenge and support when needed.

A relationship requires at least two people...working together

Work responsibilities can be dramatically different from department to department. Sometimes these differences in expectations, objectives and responsibility can promote riffs between departments and people. Logically, we all know when our departments and people work well together we are more likely to be productive and provide a greater level of service to each other, our customers and ourselves.

Why is it then in some companies there seems to be interdepartmental challenges which have existed for so long? It could be that when departments in any company clash, there has been an oversight of the true value we might offer each other if we would simply work together. No good can come from escalating conflict or indifference. Still these barriers commonly exist between departments in the workplace. In order to overcome our differences and strive together to serve a greater good, we must find some common ground on which to build the peace and productivity of teamwork. By doing so we begin to leverage ourselves into a better position for achieving our own goals and desires.

We best serve ourselves by serving others

Many people will agree that selfishness adds no value to a relationship. And yet you may know some employees who have visited other departments with one agenda in mind…their own. As managers we must accept some of the responsibility for this occasional employee behavior. We have continually focused on our team's productivity, sometimes stretching the boundaries of expectation to a point where any employee might feel pressure to produce. Our sometimes-intense management focus on the results may have encouraged some employees to feel we only care about the result and not the people. This is not true. In fact, just the opposite is true. Because we care about you, our customers and our company we strive for the highest levels of productivity in order to best serve them all. Regardless of our productivity focus, we never intended to promote interdepartmental challenges.

What we would encourage employees of every department to understand is we believe if we could all work together we would all be happier and more productive. How can this be accomplished? It can be accomplished by listening to the needs of other employees in other departments, helping them achieve their objectives, and by helping them to solve their problems. When we do this we best position them to help us with our needs and objectives. It's a "win-win" for everyone.

In any business, interdepartmental relationships are symbiotic by nature. We all need each other to do our very best in our own job so others can produce the highest level of achievement in theirs. When there is discord we all produce less. When we work in harmony we produce more. By helping other employees in other departments improve their work position we commonly create the means for them to help us, and just as important, we may enhance in them the desire to help us best fulfill our function. We best serve ourselves by serving others.

Information is power

The power to do more, the power to become more and the power to offer more to others is enhanced by the amount of information we possess. More information may not always guide us to the perfect decision, but it certainly can help us to achieve a more informed decision.

If we want to become more successful than we already are we must actively pursue information. Regardless of your role in your company, information is the fertile ground from which all of the best decisions will sprout.

We must all accept personal responsibility to seek out information that can help us to better perform our functions on the job. There are many sources that can become for you an information resource. You may find useful information in discussions with your peers. You may also find we, your managers, are a valuable information resource. Company training programs, trade magazines, the internet, the local newspaper, industry continuing education classes and field experts may all be resources which can propel your personal achievement and satisfaction to the next level. With the appropriate information and a high enough level of desire great things can be accomplished.

The more we understand a thing…the easier it becomes

Employees come to us for help, information and guidance. We do the best we can to provide them with the information and understanding we possess but sometimes it simply isn't enough. You may find this difficult to believe, but we don't know it all. We wish we did, but we don't.

We would like to solicit your help. We believe the better you understand something the easier it is for you to be productive with it. The challenge for us is, everything is changing so quickly and we have so much responsibility to our employees, company and customers that we sometimes find it difficult to be all things for all people.

We've found the most successful employees today have developed their own pool of resources they can dip into at any time to gain required information, help and support. We call these employees "Community Builders." They understand the need for accepting personal responsibility for the business environment. They work to improve communications and relationships between departments. They proactively seek new ways and new information to help them be more effective in their jobs.

They understand and believe the sharing of information, solutions and ideas makes all who wish to participate stronger, more vibrant employees and people.

The first step in developing more potent resource channels is identifying these possible future assets.

Exercise: Identifying Possible Resources

When we accept responsibility for developing our own pool of resources, we exhibit more deliberate influence over gaining answers to questions, resolving work related problems and finding ample support for our initiatives. By identifying and opening additional lines of information and support we also relieve the strained and sometimes "bottlenecked" information resources we may be too dependent on now.

The more potent information and support resources we can develop, the easier it becomes to do our job and achieve our business and personal objectives.

Instructions:

In the spaces provided create a list of people, departments and informational resources that may help you to perform your job function more effectively. (Focus more on what or whom you think might be of help to you if the resource was available. Don't focus on a person's current level of willingness to help you, but instead consider their ability to help you in some way if he/she posses the needed motivation to do so.)

Possible People Resources:

Examples:

Parents, spouse, peers, mentors, coaches, etc…

_____   _____

_____   _____

_____   _____

Possible Departmental Resources:

Examples:

Service department personnel, sales department personnel, human resource dept., marketing, customer service dept., etc…

_____   _____

_____   _____

_____   _____

Possible Information Resources:

Examples:

Trade magazines, training programs, continuing education classes, books, etc…

_____   _____

_____   _____

_____   _____

How and when will you begin to engage and utilize the possible resources you've chosen?

Resource:	What do I need to do?	When:
_____	_____	_____
_____	_____	_____
_____	_____	_____
_____	_____	_____
_____	_____	_____
_____	_____	_____

Don't forget to share with people who care about you what you're working on. Some of those same people may be in a position to help you leverage your proposed future resources more effectively, easily or quickly!

With whom will you share your intentions?

_____   _____

_____   _____

Chapter 10

Choosing Priorities

Everyone occasionally struggles with managing time these days. There always seems to be so much to do and so little available time to do it in.

Time is that quality of nature which keeps events from happening all at once. Although, lately it doesn't seem to be working!

Understanding effective time use can be a life-long pursuit. But, who really has the time to pursuit it? As if you don't have enough to do already, other people continue to bring you things they would like to see done as well. In the "hurry and get everything done" world you work in today, how can all of the priorities getting pressed upon you ever be satisfied?

Just like you, we managers are often challenged with deciding between tasks deemed by others as important, urgent, vital, key, critical, essential, or significant. These are all terms, which might be used to describe the level of value someone else has attached to the priority they expect us to serve. Just like you, we can get caught between the rock and the hard place when we attempt to serve all of the priorities presented to us at work. It can be confusing. It can be frustrating. It can be stressful.

More importantly…it can encourage anyone to lose sight of his or her own goals and job satisfaction. We'd like to help.

Time Management is really Self Management

We can't manage time. What we can manage is ourselves during any period of time. We all choose how the time we have will be used. We choose our use of time consciously or unconsciously, but we choose.

We've discovered the first step in relieving some of our time management issues at work is to identify any possible "time wasters." Time wasters are those tasks and responsibilities which can drain the minutes and hours from our already over burdened day. We're not suggesting you have the ability to eliminate all of your possible time wasters. But, by first identifying them you may be able to eliminate, or at least alleviate, some of them. Wouldn't that lessen some of the pressure on you?

 ## *Exercise: Identifying Your Time Wasters*

Identifying the major time wasters in your work life is essential to attaining maximum productivity and achieving the goals and objectives you create for yourself at work. If you can identify the things that might be draining useful work hours, then you should have time to proactively begin to make some positive headway in improving yourself, your situation at work and your overall condition in life.

Instructions:

The 25 most common time wasters in business currently are listed below. In the "Rating" column, rate each one on a scale of 1-5, indicating how much of a time waster each one is for you. If you think of any additional time wasters you don't find listed here, feel free to add and rate them at the bottom of this list. (Do not do anything with the "Impact Yes/No" area yet. We'll come back to that decision area.)

Answer Key: 5 = very significant time waster
                    1 = not a significant time waster

External Time Wasters	Rating	Impact Yes/No
Telephone Interruptions	_____	_____
Meetings Held By Others	_____	_____

Drop-in Visitors	_____	_____
Socializing	_____	_____
Lack of Information	_____	_____
Paperwork	_____	_____
Communication Breakdown	_____	_____
Lack of Policies and Procedures	_____	_____
Red Tape/Delays	_____	_____

Internal Time Wasters	**Rating**	**Impact Yes/No**
Procrastination	_____	_____
Unclear Objectives	_____	_____
Failure to Set Priorities	_____	_____
Putting Out Fires	_____	_____
Failure to Plan	_____	_____
Poor Scheduling	_____	_____
Lack of Self-discipline	_____	_____
Attempting Too Much	_____	_____
Lack of Relevant Skills	_____	_____
Unproductive Attitude	_____	_____
Fatigue	_____	_____
Over Analyzing Tasks	_____	_____
E-Mail	_____	_____
Voice Mail	_____	_____
Over Commitments	_____	_____
Lack of Priorities	_____	_____

Good job! Now that you've identified what might be the biggest time wasters for you, take time to determine and circle which ones you believe are your top 5. (It isn't important that you "stack rank" them, only that you highlight the 5 you feel cause you the greatest amount of time loss.)

Next, lets consider how all of the time in our lives actually gets used.

Priorities drive Decisions that result in Actions

Every decision one makes and every action one takes is a direct response to the priorities one possesses. Commonly, the time pressures you might experience at work are not a result of too few priorities but just the opposite, it's the result of attempting to serve too many priorities. Other people routinely bring their priorities to you. In fact, so many people may be jockeying for your time that you may actually find it difficult to decide which priorities should be addressed soon, which priorities should receive less immediate attention and which should receive no attention at all.

The challenge with serving the priorities of others is some of the priorities may be in conflict with one another. For example:

If you work in a customer service role, you may often find yourself in a situation where a customer feels they need immediate attention. What if one of your peers from another department tries to interrupt you about an unrelated issue at the same time? And what if, on top of it all, your manager requires you to make a certain number of customer contacts a day and you're running behind schedule today? Combine all of these with the probability of someone on your team calling an impromptu meeting and all of a sudden you've got a time problem. Does any of this sound familiar?

The priorities I choose drive the decisions I make, which result in the actions I take

Priorities drive decisions, which result in actions. What we believe you need is not more priorities but instead you need "One" priority. As an employee you need one priority that will always guide you to make the best decision regardless of the situation. You need one priority to help you to tread through the underbrush of pressure you sometimes endure from others and make the best decision for yourself, your customers, your team, your managers and your company.

There is one priority we have found works extremely well in helping you to serve not only yourself but also others more effectively.

Your #1 Priority should be:

I will improve my situation and myself a little every day!

When anyone dedicates consistent focus on self-improvement certain things begin to happen. First and foremost, the person can find their work easier to accomplish over time. With this self-improvement focus you better position yourself for personal goal and objective achievement. Also, you become best prepared to serve others more effectively, which improves results and reduces stress.

What we're suggesting is, when you maintain your focus on personal improvement, that focused priority influences all decisions in very positive and productive directions.

Consider the previous work example. If the referenced employee is truly focused on improving his or her situation and self a little every day then:

1. With improvement, customers receive better service.
2. Manager's productivity expectations become easier to achieve.
3. Communications with other departments are productively improved and prioritized.
4. The information received in meetings becomes more useful as it is naturally prioritized based on the impact it might have on personal improvement objectives.
5. At the end of the day, this employee will probably feel better about personal improvement, his work and himself.

Improvement is the result of Evaluation, Knowledge and Action

Simply determining what your "Time Wasters" are may not be enough. You must consider taking some action to improve your personal outcome when facing these possible time waster situations. By identifying your personal time wasters, you are now prepared to re-evaluate your work situation and discover which possible time wasters can be positively impacted.

For example:

If you rated the External Time Waster "Telephone Interruptions" highly and you are utilizing the suggested #1 Employee Priority, then you might attempt to improve your situation and yourself by:

1. Communicate more effectively with those who might call to shorten conversation time.

2. Schedule call back times rather than answering whenever your phone rings.

3. Offer voicemail options to callers so you improve telephone traffic flow.

4. Examine telephone-operating procedures with your manager to determine whether some productive changes might be implemented.

If you rated the *Internal Time Waster* "Failure to Plan" highly and you are utilizing the suggested #1 Employee Priority then you might attempt to improve yourself and your situation by:

1. Schedule and include planning as part of your regular daily activities.

2. Consult with your manager and peers to determine their effective planning procedures.

3. Refer to your "Tactical Mapping" to determine whether your daily plans and activities are helping you to achieve your goals and objectives.

4. Review your daily plans and activities with your manager to determine whether your time is being most effectively used.

Exercise: Determining Priority Impact

Priorities drive decisions, which result in actions. If you accept and follow the suggested #1 Priority, *"To improve my situation and myself a little every day"* it will have an effect on the decisions you make at work. When considering any situational decision, the contemplation of self-improvement can alter the decision to guide you in an improvement direction. The more

you improve your situation and yourself the more likely things will get easier and less stressful for you at work.

Instructions:

Part I

Review the list of common Time Wasters again.

This time ask yourself:

"*If I strive to improve myself and my situation a little every day* might I positively impact this time waster…over time?"

Answer Yes or No to each Time Waster in the "Impact Yes/No" category.

Part II

In the space provided below, list what you determined are your "top five" Time Wasters and list at least one decision or action solution you will implement to possibly eliminate or alleviate that time waster.

(Keep in mind; any improvement idea is a good idea. Try it. If it doesn't work you can always try something else.)

<u>Top 5 Time Wasters:</u>   <u>Possible Solution:</u>

1. _____   _____

                                                    _____

                                                    _____

2. _____   _____

                                                    _____

                                                    _____

3. _____   _____

_____

_____

4. _____   _____

_____

_____

5. _____   _____

_____

_____

Part III

Now pick the two of your top 5 Time Wasters you would like to first begin to improve. (Please consider sharing these choices with your manager. Your manager may be able to help you with your improvement ideas and plans.)

<u>Top 2 Time Wasters:</u>   <u>Possible Solution:</u>

1. _____   _____

_____

_____

2. _____   _____

_____

_____

Please remember two things:

1. Some improvement is better than no improvement.
2. We didn't get the way we are over night. We got the way we are over time.

Be patient with yourself and others. If you truly want improvement to happen and you're willing to work patiently at it...it will happen!

Chapter 11

Decisions That Pay

Every day we are faced with choices at work. Each of the choices we make impacts our lives, productivity and opportunities in some fashion.

My decisions determine my destiny

All decisions have consequences. As managers, we've learned every decision we make will either simplify or complicate our lives in the future. If we make any decision without considering the long-term effects, the consequences we endure are often more taxing than the original decision situation.

Likewise, if you make decisions on the job, which don't reflect your #1 Priority, you may also complicate your life and in turn diminish the satisfaction you might otherwise realize if you had maintained your focus on your "bigger" picture and #1 priority.

It's all up to me, and the decisions I make

Any employee may make hundreds of decisions at work every day. Some of them have a productive outcome and some of them don't. As you navigate through the daily routines of work you're often called on to make decisions based on shifting priorities. What's urgent and what's not? What's right and what's wrong? What's good for you and what's not? And…what will more likely influence others to be happy or unhappy?

Two motivators influence everyone. These motivators, as we've mentioned before, are the avoidance of pain and the pursuit of gain. As it relates to these two decision catalysts, certain unfortunate outcomes appear to be common.

1. When we focus only on the short-term avoidance of pain we often create for ourselves longer-term pain.

2. When we focus only on the short-term pursuit of gain we can also create for ourselves longer-term pain.

As regretful as these seemingly inevitable outcomes are, many people continue to make short term decisions because it sometimes feels more rewarding to avoid the pain of change and/or task at the moment than it does to achieve some future reward based on effective long term decision making and doing something differently.

For example:

Choosing not to accurately record and process the information of your daily work may "feel" like your cutting yourself some slack at the moment you make the choice. But, at some point those details will be needed by either you or someone else. When that information is needed and unavailable, you and others may experience pain or dissatisfaction because you neglected to record and process the information when you should have.

Short-term decisions can create long-term consequences

We are concerned for you. Our management concern stems from the knowledge that when you make "short term thinking decisions" it quite often complicates your life.

You would never consider crossing a busy highway while looking only at your feet! Of course you wouldn't. If you were crossing a busy highway you'd look across, left and right continuously until you were safely on the other side. Making "short-term thinking decisions" can create dire consequences, just like blindly crossing a busy street.

Make decisions for today, but keep tomorrow in mind

We managers have learned over time the value of making decisions from a long-term mindset. Company policy decisions must include employee, customer and cost impact considerations. Work procedure decisions must continue to reflect the longer-term outcomes we hope to produce. Even smaller, everyday decisions we make as your managers must include the long-term concerns of doing what's best for everyone involved. Would you really want us to make decisions about you and your work by only considering what the short-term consequences or rewards for us as managers might be? No, of course not. Nor would we want to.

Good intentions + good plans + good actions = Great Future

Understanding the positive and negative impact of long-term and short-term thinking is the first step in making decisions, which will improve your life, make your job easier, reduce your stress and offer you more personal satisfaction. You create your best future when you make choices and decisions based on the knowledge that your future is yours to create. Your decisions and actions, when based on priorities and plans, are much more potent than anything you might choose when simply reacting to the current conditions or environment where you work. In addition, by making good choices based on the proactive foundation of long-term thinking, you actually begin to create a future for yourself that will most likely contain less difficult choices. It's a definite "work advantage" for you. You make fewer mistakes now and, by doing so; you create a more pleasurable, productive and less stressful future!

 *Exercise: Decision Dynamics*

You make many decisions every day. If you think only in the "short-term" and not in the "long-term" you can actually complicate your own life in the near and distant future. Longer-term thinking is more productive, less stressful and helps to create for you a future more likely to yield the goals and objectives you would like to achieve.

Instructions:

Part I

Review the following decision opportunities. On the left is the "short-term" thinking approach to the decision opportunity and on the right is the "long-term" approach. Then rate yourself based on whether you feel you are more likely to choose either the short-term or long-term decision platform. These ratings range from 1-7 depending on which side of the page you most commonly make these decision choices. If you feel you are completely on the left you would give yourself a rating of 1 (one) and if you feel that you are completely on the right then you would rate yourself at a 7 (seven).

<u>Short-Term Thinking</u>   <u>Long-Term Thinking</u>

It's easier to work alone   It's better to work as a team

1	2	3	4	5	6	7

I do what I want to do   I do what I should do

1	2	3	4	5	6	7

I don't like paperwork   Information is important

1	2	3	4	5	6	7

I want people to like me   I want people to respect me

1	2	3	4	5	6	7

I stop when I'm tired   I relax when I'm finished

1	2	3	4	5	6	7

I say what others want to hear   I always tell the truth

1	2	3	4	5	6	7

I don't have time for planning   My best results occur by plan

1	2	3	4	5	6	7

It's easier not to change   Change helps me grow

1	2	3	4	5	6	7

I prefer instant gratification   I work for long-term rewards

1	2	3	4	5	6	7

Excellent! Now review your ratings. Which ones are more on the left and which are more on the right?

These are some reasons why employees are better served to use "Long-Term" thinking:

1. It is often easier to work on your own, but in the long run it's more productive to leverage yourself with other professional adults.

2. Sometimes doing what you want conflicts with doing what you should. In the long term, doing what you should do, will provide you with more future opportunity.

3. Paperwork can feel like a burden but the information that is on the paperwork makes it possible for everyone to be more successful.

4. Making a decision so someone will like you now may cost you the respect of that person later if you sacrifice what you believe is right.

5. Rewarding yourself with no work now because your tired may result in lost productivity, additional stress, time and energy later if you get behind.

6. Telling others what they want to hear instead of what you know is true may satisfy them now, but wait until they find out the truth later. Oops!

7. Not taking the time to plan will probably lead to a lot more unproductive work later.

8. Avoiding change may feel better now but changing now will make you feel a lot better later.

9. Making decisions which reward you now may cost you the much larger rewards including the satisfaction that comes from improvement and achievement.

Part II

Pick at least two-(2) decision opportunity areas you feel you could improve and list the possible benefits of your improvement in these areas.

Example:

Choosing to Plan.

Creating and working with a daily plan like I should, rather than winging it like I want to, will help me to meet my objectives every day. This will help me reduce stress, achieve my personal goals and objectives. Accomplish more work. Get along better with my manager. Help my company succeed in its mission. Create more goodwill for me from my company, manager and peers.

Long-Term Thinking Approach & Potential Benefits

1. _____

_____

_____

2. _____

_____

_____

Chapter 12

Focusing Your Energy

On what do you spend your energy each day?

My ability to achieve is improved by the energy I'm willing to contribute to my objectives

It's been said many times, "We get out of a thing what we're willing to put into it." We believe this to be true. The important question to ask is, "On what am I spending my energy?"

Each of us has an allotted amount of energy to be expended on any given day. We all work a certain number of hours. Plus, we have lives and responsibilities outside of work that require an investment of personal energy as well. Just like you, we managers sometimes go home at the end of the day feeling like one more responsibility or crisis would be more than we could stand. Let's suppose each person has a daily energy allotment of 100 energy units. If you spend 5 energy units getting ready for and going to work, and another 85 or 90 units at work, you're going to have very little energy left over for the people you care about in your personal life or the evening activities after work.

It takes more energy to be unhappy than happy

Some people spend their energy wisely others do not. If a person spends energy wisely he or she will most likely go home at the end of the day feeling satisfied and accomplished. If the energy is wasted in trivial pursuits then one's workday may be lost to frustration, aggravation and regret. Have you ever noticed when you have your most successful days at work you seem to have plenty of energy left for the other people and things important to you after work, and when you've experienced a troubling and regretful day at work you sometimes go home physically and emotionally drained? There are reasons for these conditions.

Success creates energy while frustration depletes it

Haven't you ever noticed how good you feel and how full of energy you are after you've had a productive and successful day? On the opposite side of this equation, haven't you also noticed how personally depleting it is and how much energy it takes to have a difficult and challenging day? We have. And, we have good news!

You are the master of your attitude and actions

Every person controls his or her own attitude. A person's attitude can be defined as the way one thinks, feels and acts. The way each person thinks affects the way he or she feels. The way one feels affects the way one behaves. We are all in control of what we think about so we are the masters of our attitude.

The simple truth is, when any person chooses to maintain a positive and productive attitude, units of energy rise and when a negative attitude is chosen energy units are drained. The more good things you think and do, the more good you "can" do and the more energy you have to do it. The challenge can be, you don't live or work in a vacuum. There are things happening around you all day long. Some of these events you may know are coming and some you may not. Some are deemed by you to be "positive" and others you determine to be "negative."

We are all human. Being human can sometimes make matters even more difficult. Humans are creatures capable of extraordinary empathy. We feel for others in pain or turmoil. We can relate to the misgivings or concerns of our peers. And, if we are not careful…we might not just feel for them…we might feel just like them!

Pain is an energy drain

The more negative a person feels during his or her day, the more energy gets used and the more tired and frustrated that person can become. In this condition, if you're not careful you can also become an energy drain for someone else. When that happens everyone in your immediate circle of influence may become energy depleted.

This is the way it works. It actually takes more energy to feel negatively than it does to feel positively. The more negatively a person feels the more energy depleted the person can become. Sometimes these energy-depleted people go to others and share their frustrations. Imagine that as a person's energy depletes because of a poor attitude, he or she may sometimes feel the need to draw on the energy of others in order to sustain these negative emotions. We don't believe this energy drain is always intentional but we all know it happens, don't we?

How does it encourage you to feel when someone attempts to draw you into his or her bad attitude? Frustrated? What value does it serve? Often the outcome of this exchange can be he or she feels better for a short time but you feel worse. To us, your managers, this doesn't appear to be a useful or fair exchange of time or energy. Has anyone ever done this to you? Worse yet…have you ever done this to someone else? We hope not.

No one has the right to rain on someone else's parade

We believe every manager; in fact, every employee has the responsibility to be a positive and productive role model for others on the team and in the work place. We all have the professional responsibility to lift each other up and influence our work environment for the better, not to make it worse. Doesn't your day become more frustrating and difficult when one of your peers comes to work and gives you an emotional "black eye?"

No one really knows what you must go through each day in your own life or how much effort you have to exert to create your own positive appearance and maintain your own positive attitude. We don't believe anyone has the right to come to work and rain on your parade endeavoring to make themselves feel better or draw off your energy in a vain attempt to replenish his or her own depleting energy resource. Do you? We didn't think so.

The only true control…is "Self-Control"

You can't really "make" anyone else do anything. As much as we might all sometimes like to control others, we can only truly control our self.

Control:

There are certain things in your life you can control. Let's consider your work life for a moment. Aren't there choices you make for yourself and by yourself?

Here are some examples of some of the things every person controls as it relates to work.

1. <u>Attitude</u>. No one can make us happy or unhappy. We choose happiness or unhappiness for ourselves.

2. <u>Being Prompt</u>. No one can make us late for work. Sure, occasionally something unusual happens, like an unexpected accident, but normally if we plan to leave early enough we are on time.

3. <u>Accepting Change</u>. Things change. If we are going to best accomplish our own goals we must change as well. No one can make us change. Someone can encourage or even threaten us to change, but we make the choice for ourselves.

4. <u>Having a Plan</u>. The skills and benefits of effective planning develop out of the personal desire one has for improvement and success. Others may require you to plan, but whether your plan is useful and continuous or useless and sporadic is up to you. It's another choice we all make for ourselves.

Influence:

There are certain things and people at work you may influence. There is certainly more you can influence than control. Influence is the act of encouraging others to view things and do things based on your deductions, feelings and recommendations. Sometimes you may even influence others to participate in the activities or emotions in which you would like them to engage. You influence situations and people with your thoughts, feelings and actions. In other words, you can actually influence situations and other people with your attitude. You can influence them for the better, or you can influence them for the worse. Why is this important for you to know? Because we believe you have more influence than you sometimes give yourself credit.

Some examples of a person's possible influences at work are:

1. <u>Peers</u>. We can make it easier or more difficult for others to work through their own day.

2. <u>Situations</u>. We make our situation better or worse depending on the attitude we choose for ourselves.

3. <u>Successes</u>. We achieve a lot or a little depending on our plans, attitudes and choices we make at work.

4. <u>Customers</u>. We influence others to trust and work with us or to not trust us and even work against us. We do this with our attitude and behavior.

No Control:

The largest area is the area of no control. You have no control or influence over people and things in this area. Sometimes you may wish you had control or influence over some of these things. You may even become frustrated or angry when things don't go the way you want them to. But, the fact remains; these are people and situations of no control.

Here are some examples of things people probably have little or no control over at work:

1. Company policy or procedure. There are occasions when input is asked for by the senior leadership of a company, but for the most part, the creation of company policy and procedure is out of our control.

2. Someone else's attitude. No matter how much we feel for them and how much we'd like to help, someone else's attitude is really his or her own choice. This is also true with customers, even when we are only trying to help. Each person decides what his or her attitude will be.

3. Compensation plans. Obviously, compensation plan and benefit changes can lead to some people becoming bothered or concerned. On occasion, some employees may even attempt to prevent or influence the change from occurring. Still, with rare exception, this is in an area of no control.

4. Job Descriptions/Work Responsibilities. Sometimes job responsibilities change. Whenever things like the economy, our customers, our business or our competition change we also may need to change. Defining the needs or work requirements of our role with the company is definitely an area of no personal control for many of us.

There are some words of wisdom we've learned that can help anyone to be happier and more productive in the three areas of control, influence and no control.

In areas of *Control* the words are:

Do it!

If you believe something needs to be done or changed, and you believe it to be in an area of control for you then...*do it*! Don't wait, don't hesitate, just get it done. You'll most likely feel much better when you get the change implemented, the task accomplished or the problem solved. So...*do it*!

In areas of *Influence* the words are:

Be nice!

You will consistently have more influence with others as you interact with them when you are nice. Being pushy or insensitive over a situation may make you feel better in the short term but it will most likely make the other person feel worse. So, if you want to be more successful in opportunities of influence and would even like to increase the size of your area of influence then…please be *nice* to everyone!

In areas of *No Control* the words are:

Get over it!

If you think something needs to be changed and you try to change it but you can't, it might be that the issue is actually in someone else's area of control. If this is true, your best alternative is to attempt to influence the person or the situation. Still, if you attempt to influence and you're nice and the situation still doesn't change what should you do? Our recommendation is you do what we do. *Get over it!* We've all seen other people in similar situations worry about it, fret about it and complain about it until they actually complicate matters even more. What's the value in that? As we've suggested earlier, negative emotions and attitudes are actually a drain on others and ourselves. If there is nothing you can do to change or influence the situation at the moment the best, most effective and most positive course of action is to just…*get over it!* Besides, you can always readdress the issue if you discover you're in a more influential position in the future. But for the time being, it simply makes more sense and puts you in a better position to serve your own plans if you just, for now anyway, get over it and refocus on the things you <u>can</u> control or influence.

 *Exercise: High and Low Impact*

You spend energy every day at work. If you spend your energy wisely, you reap the rewards of having plenty of energy to work and play. You can improve your opportunity to be productive and successful at work by focusing your energy on "High Impact" activities instead of "Low Impact" activities.

Keep in mind, the more successful you are at work, the greater the chance you will put yourself in a positive position to achieve your personal goals and objectives.

Instructions:

Part I

Review the list of activities below and determine whether each activity is in an area of Control, Influence or No Control for you. Write C, I or NC, (Control, Influence or No Control), for each activity to the right of the activity in the provided space.

Activity	(C) Control, (I) Influence or (NC) No Control
1. Procrastinating	_____
2. Setting priorities	_____
3. Personal/work planning	_____
4. Displaying a positive attitude	_____
5. Answering E-mail	_____
6. Attending meetings held by others	_____
7. Complaining	_____
8. Defining your work responsibilities	_____
9. Fulfilling your work responsibilities	_____
10. Completing paperwork	_____
11. Improving your abilities at work	_____
12. Listening to others complain	_____
13. Adapting to change	_____
14. Doing the "right" thing	_____
15. Being prompt	_____

Part II

High impact activities are those activities providing you with the greatest opportunities to improve your situation and/or you. These high impact activities are normally found in areas of Control first and secondly, Influence. Review the activities above again and create a list of 3 things you can do differently in the future that might allow you a greater return on your energy investment at work. Include your reason for choosing this new behavior.

For example, you might create something like this:

I will display a positive attitude even when I don't feel like doing so. I know if I attempt to think positively and act accordingly it will be better for me overall. I'll be able to get more done, I'll feel better about my work and other people will be more likely to want to help me.

1. _____

_____

_____

2. _____

_____

_____

3. _____

_____

_____

Focus consistently on the areas of personal improvement you've chosen and watch how quickly you get positive and influential results.

Chapter 13

Understanding Change

Everything appears to be changing so quickly these days. So much so, it can be difficult to know which changes are good for us, which changes are not and more importantly…who or what is to blame?

The only constant in the universe is…change

It is true that everything is changing faster today than in the past, but that doesn't necessarily mean everyone is getting better at transitioning through the changes. Change can impact anyone at anytime. It can impact people both positively and negatively. Managers and employees alike are subject to the natural emotional attachments and the decision and action influences they may encourage, when facing any change.

As managers we know you may sometimes give us more credit for the volume and speed of changes and transitions at work than we are due. We've heard employees say things like, "They're doing it to us again!" Or, "If it's not broken…don't fix it!" They say this as if we are entirely responsible for any change to which they are subjected. Yes, we are accountable for any change the organization or our team must transition through, but we may not have originated the compelling need or reason for the specific change.

Changes are like subway trains. If you don't like this one, there will be another along in a few minutes.

There are forces of change we all must be sensitive to if our business is going to thrive so we can continue to serve our customers. These forces of change are the primary reasons all businesses must consider transitioning to a new way at any given time.

5 Forces of Change

1. Customers
2. Competition
3. Technology
4. Company
5. People

If any of these 5 Forces of Change begin to alter or shift from their current condition, we must commonly adjust the way we do things so we can continue to be useful and valuable in our relationship with them. Now you might be saying to yourself, "But why do we have to change?" The answer is simple.

When faced with change, Mother Nature only allows us three options…Adapt, Migrate or Perish

Try, fly or die…these are the only choices we get when faced with inevitable change.

For example:

If our customer's business changes we have to choose. Will we change? If not, what might happen? Well, if we adapt to the change and attempt to work with our customers while they are transitioning to a new way of doing something, the relationship with them may be improved and we may be able to serve them even better as a result of our mutual change. We can ignore the customers who are changing and migrate to a new market place but if we do might we find ourselves in the same or worse condition with our new clients? Or, we can resist the changes and possibly run the risk losing our customers because they now need something different from us! Any way you look at it, changing seems to be the only logical, productive and profitable answer.

Here's another example:

The company changes because technology has changed. We are all employees. All employees including managers only have three choices. We can adapt, migrate or perish. If we adapt to the new technology and the possible changes in procedure we continue to be productive and useful in our business role and relationships at work. If we migrate and move to another company we may be fine for a while but normally technology changes will impact every business in a particular industry. So, if we migrate we may just be postponing the inevitable. Or, we can resist the change, but we may end up being swept away by the overwhelming tide that changing technology can spawn and end up losing our job after all! The only reasonable response to a technology change is to adapt.

Change is just an event

The simple truth is, change has no impact on any of us on it's own. Change is just an event. It's just another moment in your life you will most likely live through. In order to give change power over you, you must attach an emotion to it. You decide for yourself how you feel about the change. You do this unconsciously. Most commonly, you attach an emotion to a change based on what you believe this change is going to mean to you. Every time you face change you, like everyone else, reach into your imaginary pocket and pull out your personal, emotional price tag. What is this change going to mean to you? What is it going to do for you, or, what is it going to cost you? If you anticipate a positive outcome you naturally attach a positive emotion to the change. If you anticipate a negative outcome, you attach a negative emotion to the change.

What is the answer to the following question?

If a tree falls in the forest and no one is there to hear it…will it make any noise?

"Unknown"

The answer is "who cares?" There's no one there anyway. Change and emotion work the same way.

If a change happens in a different city and has no impact on you or anyone you know or care about, what does it really matter to you? We're not saying you don't care about the people the change does impact. We're suggesting that because there is no impact on you personally the change doesn't invoke an intense emotional attachment, connection or response for you. You are most dramatically impacted by those changes that happen to you, personally. You can also be emotionally impacted when change happens to those whom you care about. Maybe not as intensely, but it can definitely influence the way you feel. Understanding how change impacts you emotionally is important because the way you feel and the resulting choices, has a definite bearing on the way you behave.

Change by itself is neither positive nor negative…it's how we respond to it that determines the outcome.

Dr. William D.S. Smitley

If you feel positively about a change you will most likely take positive action. If you feel negatively about a change you will most likely take negative action or no action at all. Sometimes people even wait to see what the change might mean to them before doing anything. We call this *transition hesitation.* Still, whether you act positively, act negatively or hesitate…it is always a choice! You, like us, feel emotion when faced with some changes. How you choose to act is up to you.

I think. Therefore I feel. I feel. Therefore I act.

Our emotions are fuel for the fire of motivation. The more powerful our emotion the more spontaneous is our reaction to the situation, although we can still decide for ourselves how we are going to feel or act at any given time. If you make up your mind all changes are bad then most change will impact you negatively. When you feel this way the change will commonly be more difficult for you to implement. If you make up your mind most changes are good, it is more likely you will find a quicker and more positive personal advantage in the change. Also, the change usually becomes easier for you to implement.

"Whatever the mind can perceive the body can achieve."

Zig Zigler

Some employees still believe they have no control over the emotions they feel during a change. For some employees change is not an open door to opportunity. Some employees still view change as an endurance test, probably contrived by some manager to "shake up" the status quo. This is normally untrue. As managers, we respond to change in order to better serve our customers, employees and company in the long term. We do create change when we believe that by doing so we may better serve the team, the customers and/or the company.

Change is a natural catalyst for growth

As human beings we all grow more during times of change and transition than we do during times of no change. Think about it. As you reflect back on your own life, haven't you grown more as a direct result to change than you have when things casually remained the same? Of course you have. We all have. So, what can we all do to create a more positive outcome when facing any type of change? That's easy!

Success is a common result of creating or exploiting change

When a person is aware of the opportunities change can generate for him or her it becomes more likely that a creative way to construct a change or personally exploit a change will come to mind. When you understand and feel good about a change you get the most out of it. Believe it or not, you possess the natural ability to change and change well. Oddly enough, even those who are most resistant to change, still change. They often make matters worse. Which is by the way…change!

If you want to get the most out of your natural ability to change you can make any transition easier on yourself by following certain rules.

Transition rules:

1. **Focus on the gain!**
   There are two focus options during any transition. You can focus on the gain to be achieved or you can focus on the pain of possible personal loss. It's always a choice. Focus on the gain! The glass is either half empty or half full. Always imagine yourself working to fill up the glass. In a dramatically changing business world you can help to guarantee your own success by staying positive and focused on helping yourself and others through any change. Focus on the gain! In this way you are more likely to uncover the personal benefits that may result from the change.

2. **Make a personal investment!**
   Success is always going to take the effort of a personal investment. We've all heard, "If it's going to be…it's up to me!" Participating in the change makes you feel better. You normally feel better when you are attempting to help rather than hinder. There is hardly ever a change that couldn't use some refinement or polishing to make it even better. Ask yourself "What can I do to help?" Improvement is everyone's responsibility. We all need to

make sure when possible, things work better and faster. It's best for all, but most importantly, it's best for you.

3. **Work the change!**
You're in charge of your responses to change. You choose what you will focus on and therefore how you will feel. Look for opportunity in every change and you allow yourself a chance to be successful. Support co-workers in their attempts to deal with change. We must all embrace and work the transition in order to better serve our customers and grow our company. By doing so, we secure our own personal growth and future success. This is one way we all help ourselves to achieve our own successful future.

 *Exercise: Understanding Change Impact*

Everyone is more happy and productive when they develop a positive outlook with regard to any change. Once you understand the connection between the emotions you feel and the way feelings can encourage you to behave, it becomes easier for you to choose the most productive emotions when transitioning through change in the future.

Instructions:

Part I

List what you believe are the 3 most important change situations you have encountered at work in the last 6 months.

Changes:

1. _____

2. _____

3. _____

Part II

List your changes again and then select an emotion from the list that best describes what you felt when you found out about the impending change. (Be honest with yourself. Select the emotion that "best" describes what you felt at the time.)

<u>Change:</u>   <u>My Emotion:</u>

1. _____   _____

2. _____   _____

3. _____   _____

<u>Emotion List:</u>

Optimism	Denial	Skepticism
Misgivings	Doubt	Fear
Confusion	Withdrawal	Bailout
Hope	Enthusiasm	Commitment
Focus	Confidence	Ownership
Elation	Defiance	Resistance

Part III

List your three change situations one last time and describe your actions and how they related to how you felt in each situation.

Change	My Emotion	My Resulting Actions
1.		
2.		
3.		

If the emotion's you choose and felt at the time had been different, would the possible personal decisions and outcomes have changed as well?

Please consider your findings here as you face inevitable change in the future.

We're not suggesting a simple change of emotion and attitude is always enough to make your life less complicated at work. But, we do know looking for the gain in any change and the resulting positive attitude about the change will be far more helpful than the alternative. And, if given the opportunity, we'd like to help you through future changes as well.

Feel free to call on us for help if you need it!

Chapter 14

Working With Change

Change has always been with us. Since the beginning of time, things have changed. So why can change cause so many problems today?

Emotion is "energy in motion"

Transitioning through change is an emotional process. Sometimes change invokes strong emotion, and yet, other times it barely registers a thought. Still, the emotions of change are always with us. The speed and intensity of the changes we create and endure can contribute to the number of negative emotions we feel. The most common reason for this is the more significant and/or frequently the changes, the more difficult transitioning can become for us. The point is, when subjected to multiple or significant transitions, people sometimes may need help to effectively change.

$$\frac{\textit{Intensity of Change}}{\textit{Our Ability to Change}} = \textit{Transition Resources Needed}$$

Just like with any personal transition, we all sometimes need help during times of change. Most people would offer a friend a helping hand or meaningful advice during a personal crisis without a second thought. Many people seek help from their family and friends when facing difficult changes in their personal lives like the loss of a job, a struggling relationship, financial concerns and investment opportunities. And yet, when at work, people commonly struggle with change or improvement without asking for positive help from others to advance the prospect of success. And, things can get worse…

Misery loves company

When people feel negatively toward something it actually hurts! When facing an impending change someone else created, a multitude of negative emotions can be caused. We can feel denial or skepticism. We can feel confusion or withdrawal. When you feel negatively about a change you shouldn't search out others who also feel negatively. Or worse yet, you must not allow yourself to contribute to the negative emotions others might feel when transitioning through change. As your managers we are concerned for you. We know how painful some changes can feel at first. And yet, we also know if you bond with others who are also feeling negative emotions and pain two things can happen.

1. The pain grows

Emotion can be contagious. Haven't you ever noticed when you feel good other people around you sometimes feel better and when you feel badly others sometimes feel worse? That's what empathy is. It's understanding at some level what others are feeling and feeling for them or sometimes with them. The difficulty in this case is, if two negative people get together and share their woe, the pain grows and the transition can grind to a complete stop. You might become resistant or even defiant. There's hardly ever an "upside" for any person in this negative emotional state. Your life on the job becomes more difficult, our lives as managers become more complicated and everyone involved, including other employees, and our customers may suffer.

2. The transition slows

If you understand the "Forces of Change" and the responsibility we, as managers, have to answer to these forces with responsible and competitive improvement, then you must understand we have to do our best to ensure successful transition implementations in the workplace. We have concern for any employee who sacrifices his or her best interest in order to resist inevitable change. We've been through it too. We know how difficult it can be to change when every fiber of your mind and body want to keep doing things the "old way." But if we are all to remain in the best position to serve others and ourselves we must change as things around us change. It's not that we don't care about you…it's that we do care!

The improvement of people, plans and process creates opportunity for all

As the things around you change, you must also change. If you don't, you risk becoming stagnant and your opportunities disappear. We have all heard stories about companies that didn't change well. Many of these companies and their employees suffered significant and costly losses because of the inability or lack of desire to change. Attempting to hold back the waves of change is like attempting to make time stand still. Unfortunately, you either find some way to create or exploit change or you become engulfed in the new world change has created for you.

Will you go willingly into your new future or will it be thrust upon you? It's your choice.

When the new future arrives will you have made a happy place for yourself in it, or will you be wondering why life has become so difficult? We want all employees to make their own choices. We always hope you will survive and even thrive in the new way of any change. We want to help.

Opportunity and regret reside in every change

In order for you to take best advantage of any change situation you'll find transitioning easiest if you follow the 5 steps to effective personal transition. Please consider making the change and resulting transition easier on yourself.

1. **Try to understand the need for a "New Way."**
   People generally feel better about a change when they understand "why" a change must take place. Try to remember the goal for changing in business is not to make things different but to make things better. We're not intentionally attempting to make your life more difficult; we're attempting to answer the need the "Forces of Change" create. Keep an open mind. Consider the relationship you have with your peers and us. The more one attempts to understand the need for a new way the more likely a person will feel a positive emotion rather than a negative one. We'll try to help. We'll pass information about any change as soon as we have it. We'll listen to your implementation concerns and improvement ideas. We'll work with you to help you implement changes as quickly and effectively as possible.

And, if you don't understand, please ask us! We want changes to be easier for you, not more difficult.

2. **Identify any personal opportunity in the change.**
   As the saying goes, "Every cloud has a silver lining." Look for the silver lining in the cloud of change. In most cases, when you view a change through the positive state of personal opportunity, the change appears more viable and the opportunities for you in the change become more apparent. Ask yourself, "How can I get the most out of this change?" "How can I improve my situation by working <u>with</u> this change?" Identify some personal opportunity in the change and if you have difficulty with this, come to us and let us help you. Our work experience may provide you some insight you've not yet discovered on your own.

3. **Identify any positive or opposing forces.**
   In any transition there can be "positive" or "opposing" forces at work within the change. Do your best to identify these forces. Some people will view the change positively. Some may view it negatively. Let yourself be drawn to the positive people. Align yourself with those who feel positive about any situation and you may enhance the positive outlook you both have, making the opportunities in change more easily identifiable.
   If you struggle with this at all, please come to us and allow us to help.

4. **Develop an implementation plan.**
   Figure out what steps you must take to reap the most personal benefit from each change. What 3 things can you do to help you capitalize on the current transition? How can you feel more positive about the change? What actions can you take which would best align with your chosen positive emotions? Develop a plan that includes at least your next 2 steps and take action! Haven't you ever noticed working with something normally feels better than working against it? Negatively working against change depletes energy. Positively working with change creates energy! If you find any level of difficulty in positively working with change, please come to us.

5. **Invest energy in yourself and others.**
   Look for ways the change can help you with your personal improvement. Focus on the personal gain and work to help others see the positive opportunities in the change. A team is more than a reasonably cooperative group of people. A team helps each other through difficulty, and, because of that kind of mutual support; a team enjoys success even more. If you help a

teammate who might be struggling this time, maybe he or she will be better prepared to help you when you're in need in the future. Remember we're all in this together. There are people on the job who look up to you. There are those who watch to see what you are going to do before they make their final decisions about some changes. Let's all try to make any transition as easy on others and us as possible. Invest energy in yourself by staying focused on the gain and taking positive action. And, let's help others in their attempts to deal with change. Remember: Most changes involve other people. Let's work together!

By following these 5 steps to effective personal transition you not only help yourself…you help others. We've all heard before, "Change is good!" We know all change doesn't always initially feel "good." But we also know if we all work together to feel more positive about every change, the inevitable outcomes and personal rewards for everyone involved are normally much greater. Why? Because we can help to lift each other up and create the critical mass necessary to take best advantage of any change coming our way!

 *Exercise: Working With Change*

A person's emotions can limit or improve the opportunity to be most successful when encountering change. When we take a positive emotional approach to change we are usually more productive and the opportunities created are more apparent and achievable. When we take a negative approach the outcome produced is usually less productive and less gratifying. In this exercise you will determine if there is an "upside" to a positive emotional approach when transitioning.

Instructions:

Examine these specific change situations and determine the possible outcomes for both the positive and negative emotional approach to each situation. Write down the possible outcomes you develop for each suggested situation.

Example:

<u>A new procedure that requires changing your work routines</u>

<u>Emotions</u>	<u>Possible Outcomes</u>
Optimism, Hope	It will be easier for me to find personal opportunity in the change. I will be in a better frame of mind to help others if they struggle. I will feel better. I will be happier. Little things won't bother me as much.
Skepticism, Fear	I could resist the change. I might complicate my life at work. I might make it more difficult for others to change. I could jeopardize the relationship I have with my manager, my peers and/or my customers. I will most likely feel more stress and tension than I would like to.

Change	Emotions	Possible Outcomes
A new procedure that requires changing your work routines.	Optimism, Hope	
	Skepticism, Fear	
Getting a new team leader or manager.	Enthusiasm, Commitment	
	Denial, Misgivings	
Being asked to improve your work skills.	Focus, Confidence	
	Doubt, Resistance	

Doesn't this exercise solidify the concept that positive emotions are more likely to enable positive results and negative emotions are more likely to enable negative results?

Looking for the positive outcome in any change is not always easy. But we know when you attempt to look for the positive opportunities in change things normally seem to work out better for you.

Focus on the possible gain in any change. Be aware of your emotions and how negative emotions can encourage you to act. Help others in their attempts to deal with change and if needed, please come to us for help.

Thank you!

Chapter 15

Creating Change

Today, more than ever, we all need to feel a stronger sense of control. There are so many people who ask so much of us all on the job it can become challenging to do everything asked of us and maintain our own personal focuses of growth, improvement, opportunity and satisfaction. Part of the reason for this personal "black hole" is the requirement at work to participate in the changes others create. As employees, we can spend so much time serving the objectives and agendas of others that we may find it challenging to initiate positive changes in our own lives. If we're not careful, we may find ourselves so busy implementing the changes others create that we may feel we don't have the time or energy to create positive change for ourselves. This can contribute to a state or feeling of victimization.

In a world full of individuals…it's easy to feel alone

We shouldn't blame others for focusing on their needs or goals. And we certainly shouldn't feel victimized when other people rely on our skills and abilities to achieve their desires. Still, the challenge is to maintain a personal sense of control and recognize we too have the need for the personal satisfaction, which only comes with chosen and earned personal achievement.

When changing at the speed of light…we're quite often in the dark

There has been a lot of information passed along over the last few years about the importance of, the reasons for and even the steps to effective personal change. As managers we are glad so many have taken an interest in this topic, because as leaders and employees, we deal with the issues of change almost every day. Nearly everyone will agree that when change is created for the purpose of improvement, it is a good thing. Still, we have learned that not everyone changes well every time and there are some very natural deterrents or stumbling blocks to personal change.

These are some of the more common obstacles that encourage people to resist change.

Change Obstacles:
1. The purpose or reasons for the change are not made clear.
2. You are not involved in the decision to change.
3. You feel group work habits and routines have been ignored.
4. Not enough information about the expected implementation.
5. Fear of failure.
6. You feel there is excessive work pressure.
7. You view the cost as too high or the reward as too low.
8. The present situation seems satisfactory to you.
9. You are not asked to participate in refining the implementation.
10. The change direction and final outcome are unclear.

As managers we are constantly working to improve our organizational and individual transition skills so we can help you through some of the more difficult changes at work. We are not suggesting we're great at it, or that we always offer change in the way everyone around us feels is the right way, but we're trying to help...not hurt. And, we'd like to help you.

Change is speeding up

We don't believe the changes you face in the workplace are ever going to slow down. In fact, based on current trends in business, our assumption is that the need to change is going to become even more frequent in the future. With this in mind we'd like offer some thoughts and suggestions about how you might help yourself to get more out of your work, your business relationships and change.

I've seen the monster...and I am he!

Bela Lugosi (1938)

We know that learning to change quickly and effectively are skills that can be developed just like any other skill. With learning to perfect any new skill there can be setbacks and challenges. Most commonly when learning to do anything new or better, people can be their own worst enemy. People often stand on their own "air hose" of improvement when overwhelmed with concern. Most generally referred to simply as "fear," there are actually 5 different fears that can slow down or stop a person's progress when attempting to create or implement change.

According to psychologist Dr. Dennis O'Grady, the inability to change is commonly associated with a possible combination of these five fears:

1. Fear of the Unknown
   (Concern that when change occurs, you will loose control)

2. Fear of Failure
   (If you commit yourself to goals for change, there is a chance for failure)

3. Fear of Commitment
   (Concern over eliminating other options, which may present themselves later)

4. Fear of Disapproval
   (Concern for what others might feel or say when you change or when they must change because of your changes)

5. Fear of Success
   (Concern about the additional demands on you as a result of your successful change, and questioning whether the newfound success is sustainable)

We have nothing to fear but fear…itself.

Franklin D. Roosevelt

Any fear can be a painful endeavor. When these 5 fears start to cause friction in your personal gears of change the sparks can fly and the transition can slow down or grind to a halt. We'd like to help you to overcome these fears. We'd like to aid you in your goals of higher levels of achievement, opportunity and growth. In order to do this, please allow us to offer you some relevant questions that might help you, as they have helped us, to jumpstart your journey on the road to personal change and improvement.

Proactive Change Questions:
1. What trends and forces of change are currently affecting my profession?
2. How can my job or responsibilities be impacted by these changes?
3. What skills and abilities do I possess or need to make these changes?
4. Which of these skills or abilities will help me continue to be successful in the future?
5. What skills do I need to stay valuable in my role?
6. What have I learned in the last six months that might help me with the change?
7. What do I expect to learn in the next six months?
8. Who might I leverage with to help me change and improve?

By occasionally reviewing these questions you can proactively put yourself in a better position to implement changes thrust upon you, and you can illuminate change opportunity you may desire to create for yourself.

The most wonderful future is the one we create

Anyone can become frustrated with change. But the people who succeed most often and are receiving the highest levels of reward and satisfaction are those who not only implement the changes others bring them but also create improvement for themselves.

Creating positive change in yourself and for yourself is the way you can take personal control and responsibility for your own happiness. It helps you to keep life interesting and challenging. It allows you to keep yourself sharp, balanced and alert. Most importantly, it reminds you that you in charge of your own fate, your own future.

I am the creator and master of my destiny

Exercise: Creating Change at Work

People are happier and more successful when they continuously strive to improve themselves, their business relationships and their work environment. We are all so busy we sometimes forget to lift our heads up from the daily work tasks and look around to determine whether we should initiate some change. When we do take the time to find the need for and initiate change, we frequently feel personally gratified as well as improve our opportunities at work. By creating needed change at work we can improve ourselves, our own situation as well as quite often improve the situation for others.

Instructions:

From the list that follows, pick 3 areas you feel, with some personal change, you might make improvement. Then write down at least one "go-forward" commitment for yourself explaining what you will change or do in each area to make this improvement. Next, make a note of any obstacles you think might attempt to derail you from your chosen improvement path and make note of anything you can think of which might eliminate these possible obstacles. Last, determine and write down the date you will evaluate your improvement in each area.

Possible Improvement Areas:

1. My work team

2. My customers

3. Other department's employees

4. My attitude

5. Vendor relationships

6. My manager/supervisor

7. Other department's managers

8. My job related skills

9. My work related knowledge

10. My productivity

Improvement Area	"Go-Forward" Commitment	Possible Obstacles	Plans to Overcome Obstacles	Improvement Evaluation Date
1.				
2.				
3.				

Please consider sharing with us any improvement areas you've chosen for yourself and allow us to help with your plans and/or implementations for those improvements.

You're not alone. Others care about you. We care about you.

We're on your side!

The Final Plan

Action Mapping

As you move forward toward your own improvement, achievement and happiness we believe you'll find this statement is true:

The most important commitments you'll ever make...are the commitments you'll make to yourself

We sincerely appreciate the time, thought and effort you've applied to this book and it's exercises. Choosing to read and work through this book took commitment. Choosing to take more control of your future and do the right things to achieve it takes character. We know you possess both of these qualities and as your managers we're extremely grateful you do. Every person's life around you is improved, as you become an even better person and employee. Most importantly, your personal commitment to excellence is the most valuable commitment any one can make!

We'd like to help you insure the work you've done affords you the highest possible levels of benefit. In order to help you realize the maximum potential from your good work, we'd like to offer you this thought:

The true purpose of education is application

These final pages are dedicated to the idea that if we can help you create a mechanism to activate and track the hard work and good intentions you've put forth as you worked through this book, we might assist you in creating your best possible future.

Many people read self-help books, listen to audios or attend classes and experience or discover ideas and concepts that might be of use to them personally. The

103

sometimes, sad reality of life is very few of these same people ever implement any of the things they've learned for the sustained, long term.

All books, audios and classes contain information. If one retains the information it becomes knowledge. If one uses this knowledge it becomes application, and if one uses the application long enough for the betterment of one's self or others it can become a valuable skill. Our hope is to help you move from information to skill as quickly, effectively and painlessly as possible.

To this end we offer you this Action Map!

Action Map: (definition—A tool used to focus, apply and track one's efforts toward improvement and achievement)

In order for this Action Map to take shape and generate power you'll need to review your work in previous chapters, make some timetable decisions and consistently review the Action Map to list and/or reevaluate your conclusions and outcomes.

Exercise: Action Mapping

Instructions:

Review the exercises you've completed in the previous chapters and complete the Action Map with the appropriate information, decisions and choices.

Action Map

Reference: Chapter One – Dreams List		
In the spaces provided below list the two "Dreams" you find most inspiring and motivational.		
My Dreams	**What actions will I take to make this dream a reality?**	**When will I do these things?** *(List expected time lines or dates)*
1.		
2.		
Reference: Chapter Two – Career Map		
In the space provided below review, finalize, and rewrite your Career Strategy (This second version may change based on additional thoughts you may have after completing this book.)		

Reference: Chapter Three – Tactical Mapping

In the spaces provided below recreate your Tactical Map
(With new information, plans can change. It's O.K. if yours do too!)

List One of Your Long-Term Goals and the Date for completion	List your Short-Range objectives that will take you closer to your goal	List any Obstacles that might hinder you're goal attainment	How will you overcome these Obstacles?

Chapter Three – Tactical Mapping (Continued)

List your personal Strengths	List your personal Improvement Opportunities	What Visualization Aids will you use to help you stay focused on your goals?

Reference: Chapter Four – Why and How do I work?	
In the spaces provided please answer the following questions:	
What are your specific motivations for working?	
What will you work to improve in order to become more effective at your job?	

Reference: Chapter Five – MVP Behaviors	
In the spaces provided below, list the two MVP Behaviors you will work to improve and the possible personal benefits of making these improvements.	
# 1 MVP Behavior:	
#2 MVP Behavior:	

Reference: Chapter Six – Embracing Improvement

In the spaces provided below, please list two of the personal improvement areas you've chosen for yourself, with whom you will share your improvement objectives with and what benefits will you receive resulting from these improvements. (Improvement areas may include: personal study, personal development, relationship development, etc...)

Personal Improvement Areas:	With whom will you share these objectives?	What benefits will you receive from these personal improvements?
1.		
2.		

Reference: Chapter Seven – Leveraging For Success

In the spaces provided below, list the actions, commitments and changes you're willing to make in order to better meet the expectations of others in the workplace and improve your relationship with them.

Actions, Commitments & Changes:

1.

2.

3.

Reference: Chapter Eight – Mutual Commitments

In the spaces provided below, list the areas of focus and improvement you and your manager agreed upon and what your next steps will be.

Improvement Areas:	Next Steps Toward Improvement:
1.	
2.	
3.	

Reference: Chapter Nine – Identifying Possible Resources

In the spaces below, list the possible resources that may help you to perform your job function more effectively.
(People, Departments and Informational resources)

1. _____	4. _____
2. _____	5. _____
3. _____	6. _____

Reference: Chapter Ten – Identifying Time Wasters

In the spaces provided below, please list your top two Time Wasters and your proposed possible solutions.

Time Waster:	Possible Solutions:
1.	
2.	

Reference: Chapter Eleven – Decision Dynamics

In the spaces provided below, please list your two chosen Decision Opportunity Areas and the benefits of improving these areas

Long-Term Thinking Approach	Potential Benefits
1.	
2.	

Reference: Chapter Twelve – High Impact Activities

In the spaces provided below, list the three things you can do differently in the future that might allow you a greater return on your energy investment at work.
(Include your reason for choosing this new behavior.)

1.
2.
3.

Reference: Chapter Thirteen – Change/ Emotional Impact

In the spaces provided below, please list two changes you're currently experiencing at work, the emotion best describing how you feel about the change and the way this emotion will encourage you to act.

Current Change	Current Emotion	Behavioral Impact
1.		
2.		

Reference: Chapter Fourteen – Leveraging Change

In the space provided below, please explain what the possible benefits are to experiencing and exhibiting positive emotions during any change or transition.

Reference: Chapter Fifteen – Possible Improvement Areas

In the spaces provided below, list the three improvement areas, "Go-forward" Commitments, possible Obstacles, Plans to Overcome Obstacles you've chosen to work on and the Dates you expect to Evaluate your Improvements in these areas.

Improvement Area	"Go-Forward" Commitment	Possible Obstacles	Plans to Overcome Obstacles	Improvement Evaluation Date
1.				
2.				
3.				

Quick Quote Reference Guide

Introduction

- ❖ Our potential is the foundation on which success can be built
- ❖ You don't know what you don't know…you know?
- ❖ Success is nothing more than the inevitable outcome of a life lived to it's fullest potential

Chapter 1—Dare to Dream

- ❖ A successful person will take responsibility for what needs to be done…and do it
- ❖ Finding answers involves understanding the questions
- ❖ Undefined and unwritten dreams fade away
- ❖ When we produce work focused on only short-term gain we often create for ourselves long-term pain
- ❖ Dreams fuel the desire to persevere through hardship
- ❖ We're all more capable than we know
- ❖ A life without dreams becomes hardship
- ❖ "Whatever we vividly imagine, ardently desire, sincerely believe and enthusiastically act upon must inevitably come to pass."

Anonymous

Chapter 2—Creating Your Future

- ❖ When you don't know where you're going…all roads lead there.

Paraphrased—Lewis Carroll

- ❖ We are all moving toward our future. We will go happily and willingly, or we will go kicking and screaming. But, we're all going.

❖ What do I expect to get out of the relationship I have with this company? And, am I getting what I need in order to be happy? If not, what am "I" doing about it?

Chapter 3—Planning For Success

❖ Vision + Planning + Competent Effort = Results

❖ Success doesn't come to you…you go to it!

❖ A one thousand-mile journey begins with a single step

Chinese Proverb

❖ Motivation is "internal" not "external"

❖ Anything you think about long enough and hard enough is bound to come true

Chapter 4—The Value of Position Descriptions

❖ Good work today…fuels tomorrow

❖ Conflict is the mother of disaster

❖ The more detailed the map…the easier the journey

❖ Future opportunity is created by current success

❖ Challenge is inevitable…winning is an option

Chapter 5—Winning Behavior

❖ Everything of value we will ever accomplish, will in some way…involve other people

❖ Indifference kills relationships

❖ I am responsible for 50% of all my relationships

❖ I am responsible for 100% of my behavior

❖ The respect of others is earned by our behaviors

❖ Change the way you think and act toward others and watch how quickly they change the way they think and act toward you.

Paraphrased—James Allen

Chapter 6—The Greatest Gift

❖ The only real improvement is "self improvement"

❖ Whatever you fill your mind with, and focus yourself on, is what you become

❖ Anything you think about long enough and hard enough is bound to come true

❖ Success is more a result of attitude than aptitude

❖ Improvement is the greatest gift we can give to ourselves

❖ Success is a road always under construction

Chapter 7—Successful Leveraging

❖ The easiest way to be successful in the future is…together

❖ A load is more easily moved when everyone pulls in the same direction

❖ We win or lose…together

❖ Teamwork creates momentum for success

❖ Mutual commitment is the bond that binds effective teams

❖ TEAM: Together Everyone Achieves More

Unknown

❖ Synergy: (definition—The combined effort is greater than it's parts.)

Chapter 8—Mutual Commitments

❖ The most important stride toward success is a commitment to personal excellence

❖ "Lord, grant that I might always desire more than I can accomplish."

Michelangelo

❖ "A man can alter his life by altering his thinking."

William James

❖ We must choose the challenges of achievement or the challenges of getting by

❖ By helping others, we help ourselves

Chapter 9—Developing Resources

❖ A smart man isn't one who knows all of the answers...A smart man is one who knows where to look for the answers.

❖ A relationship requires at least two people...working together

❖ We best serve ourselves by serving others

❖ Information is power

❖ The more we understand a thing...the easier it becomes

Chapter 10—Choosing Priorities

❖ Time is that quality of nature which keeps events from happening all at once. Although, lately it doesn't seem to be working!

❖ Time Management is really Self Management

❖ Priorities drive Decisions that result in Actions

❖ The priorities I choose drive the decisions I make, which result in the actions I take

❖ An Employee's #1 Priority should be:
   I will improve my situation and myself a little every day!

❖ Improvement is the result of Evaluation, Knowledge and Action

Chapter 11—Decisions That Pay

❖ My decisions determine my destiny

❖ It's all up to me, and the decisions I make

❖ Short-term decisions can create long-term consequences

❖ Make decisions for today, but keep tomorrow in mind

❖ Good intentions + good plans + good actions = Great Future

Chapter 12—Focusing Your Energy

❖ My ability to achieve is improved by the energy I'm willing to contribute to my objectives

❖ It takes more energy to be unhappy than happy

❖ Success creates energy while frustration depletes it

❖ You are the master of your attitudes and actions

❖ Pain is an energy drain

❖ No one has the right to rain on someone else's parade

❖ The only true control…is "Self-Control"

Chapter 13—Understanding Change

❖ The only constant in the universe is…change

❖ Changes are like subway trains. If you don't like this one, there will be another along in a few minutes.

❖ When faced with change, Mother Nature only allows us three options…Adapt, Migrate or Parish

❖ Change is just an event

❖ If a tree falls in the forest and no one is there to hear it…will it make any noise?

Unknown

❖ Change by it's self is neither positive nor negative…it's how we respond to it that determines the outcome.

Dr. William D.S. Smitley

❖ I think. Therefore I feel. I feel. Therefore I act.

❖ Whatever the mind can perceive the body can achieve.

Zig Zigler

❖ Change is a natural catalyst for growth.

❖ Success is a common result of creating or exploiting change

Chapter 14—Leveraging Change

❖ Emotion is "energy in motion"

❖ Intensity of Change > Our Ability to Change = Transition Resources Needed

❖ Misery loves company

❖ The improvement of people, plans and process creates opportunity for all

❖ Will you go willingly into your new future or will it be thrust upon you? It's your choice.

❖ Opportunity and regret reside in every change

Chapter 15—Creating Change

❖ In a world full of individuals…it's easy to feel alone

❖ When changing at the speed of light…we're quite often in the dark

❖ I've seen the monster…and I am he!

Bela Lugosi (1938)

❖ We have nothing to fear but fear…itself

Franklin D. Roosevelt

❖ The most wonderful future is the one we create

❖ I am the creator and master of my destiny

The Final Plan—Action Mapping

❖ The most important commitments you'll ever make…are the commitments you'll make to yourself

❖ The true purpose of education is application

❖ Action Map: (definition—A tool used to focus, apply and track one's good intentions toward improvement and achievement)

Research References:

The Herman Trend Alert; by Roger Herman and Joyce Gioia; September 17, 2003, The Herman Group; copyright 1998-2006.

Well-Being, Insecurity and the Decline of American Job Satisfaction; David G. Blanchflower, Dartmouth College and the National Bureau of Economic Research in cooperation with Andrew J. Oswald, University of Warwick, UK. Published April 1999 and presented to Cornell University conference May 1999.

Yerkes-Dodson Law (First observed by Robert M. Yerkes and John D. Dodson, *The Relation of Strength of Stimulus to Rapidity of Habit Formation* (1908) *Journal of Comparative Neurology and Psychology.*

As A Man Thinketh, James Allen (1864-1912) James Allen Wisdom Series, Laurel Creek Press, Third Printing 2004.

The Principles of Psychology (1890), *The Will To Believe and Other Essays in Popular Philosophy* (1897), both written by William James.

Civil Disobedience and Other Essays to include Life Without Principle (1863), Henry David Thoreau. Dover Thrift Editions

Taking the Fear out of Changing (1993), Dr. Dennis O'Grady, Adams Media Corporation; 1st edition (November, 1993).

The Emperor's Handbook: A new translation of the Meditations of Marcus Aurelius, Emperor of Rome, 121–180, (Including Ethics, Stoics and Life) C. Scot Hicks and David V. Hicks; English translation copyright 2002; Scribner Publishing, New York.

978-0-595-39432-6
0-595-39432-9